monsoonbooks

PENANG UNDERCOVER

Ewe Paik Leong is a member of International Thriller Writers in Eureka, CA, USA. His novel, *A China Doll in KL*, was nominated for the POPULAR-The Star Readers' Choice Award 2015. His nonfiction works *Kuala Lumpur Undercover* and *Kuala Lumpur Undercover II* are local bestsellers. Ewe earned his BSBA from the nationally-accredited Southwest University, Kenner, LA, USA. He lives in Kuala Lumpur with his family.

T0097181

Penang
Undercover

EWE PAIK LEONG

monsoon

monsoonbooks

First published in 2018
by Monsoon Books Ltd
www.monsoonbooks.co.uk

No.1 Duke of Windsor Suite, Burrough Court,
Burrough on the Hill, Leics. LE14 2QS, UK.

ISBN (paperback): 978-1-912049-42-4
ISBN (ebook): 978-1-912049-43-1

Cover design by Cover Kitchen.

A Cataloguing-in-Publication data record is available from the British
Library.

Printed and bound in Great Britain by Clays Ltd, Elcograf S.p.A.
20 19 18   1 2 3 4 5

Contents

1 Johns on Rickshaws   9

2 Jaunts by Rickshaw   29

3 Born-Again Devotees   48

4 Happy-Ending Massage   82

5 Gigolo Escapades   95

6 Mamasans of Patpong   110

7 Passage to Hell   135

8 Bargirls of Patpong   157

9 Hatyai's Night Butterflies   181

10 Kuala Lumpur Potpourri   204

1

Johns on Rickshaws

Forty-year-old Ah-Chye steers his trishaw to the side of Penang Road outside Cosmo Hotel (not its real name) and dismounts. He bumps its three wheels up the concrete curb, which is two inches higher than the road, and yanks on the handbrake. He dismantles the umbrella, closes its canopy and secures it to the crossbar of the trishaw. Leaning against the saddle, he waits for prospective passengers from the hotel, his gaze focused on the entrance.

Soon, a Japanese man and a Chinese girl in her early twenties emerge from the hotel and walk down to the road. As they start to scan their surroundings, Ah-Chye takes quick steps towards them. "Trishaw, sir?" he says to the Japanese man. *Looks like he's in his mid-forties.* "How about a tour? I give you special price, forty ringgit one hour."

The Japanese man says to the Chinese girl, "I haven't ridden a trishaw before. It'll be fun."

"Be adventurous, dear, and experience new things. I know a place where you can buy durians. You've to eat at the stall as they are not allowed to be brought back to hotels."

They climb aboard and Ah-Chye heads the trishaw north to make a loop around Lebuh Farquhar to proceed to the old quarter. After passing a few old Gothic-style churches, Ah-Chye overhears the Chinese girl say, "Yuta, you want to eat Chinese street food or Japanese food?"

"I would prefer Penang food."

The Chinese girl turns her head to face Ah-Chye. "Go to Lebuh Kimberley."

Ah-Chye leans forward on the handlebar. "Yes, Miss." Minutes later, he stops his trishaw outside Bee Hooi Kopitiam, a food court, and the couple gets out.

Yuta asks Ah-Chye, "You want part payment first?"

"I'll collect payment at the end of the ride, sir." Ah-Chye parks his trishaw nearby, his gaze trailing the couple as they enter the food court. A minute later, they come out and seat themselves at one of the roadside tables. The girl goes to order food from three separate hawker stalls and returns to the table. *Ho say liao! They're eating several dishes, will take a longer time.*

When they return to the trishaw, Ah-Chye overhears Yuta say, "It's time for my durian, Amy."

Amy tells Ah-Chye, "Go to Macalister Road."

During the journey, Ah-Chye overhears Amy telling Yuta about durians, "Popular species here are *ang haeh, ang sim* and *mor sang ong.* Balik Pulau is famous for durians, but the orchards impose a minimum spend for visitors. Otherwise we can visit it tomorrow. Do you know that a durian is an aphrodisiac?"

"Oh really?" Yuta releases a guffaw and places a hand on her lap. "In that case, I must eat more!"

"Then you can extend your booking!" Her fingers clasp his hand loosely. "But let's see whether you can stand the smell of durians or not?"

Ah-Chye pricks up his ears. *She's a social escort, must be a lao jiao [veteran] in George Town since she's familiar with the city.*

In Macalister Road, a cart on wheels displaying a banner that says "Penang Ah Teik Durian" is standing at the roadside. The brakes of Ah-Chye's trishaw screech to a halt at the stall and Yuta and Amy get out. Ah-Chye pushes his trishaw to a gap between two nearby hawker food stalls and waits.

Fifteen minutes later, Yuta and Amy return to the trishaw.

"Where to next?" asks Yuta, covering his mouth as he releases a burp.

"How about Slippery Senoritas?" Amy gives Yuta a sideways glance. "Just now when we passed it, I saw a sign that says it's Ladies Nights tonight."

"No, I don't want to dance."

"There's a rooftop bar in Chulia Street. Great views of the city."

"Sure, why not?"

Next morning ...
The morning-shift receptionist is checking the reservations for the day on the computer when her telephone rings.

"Hello? Front desk."

"My boyfriend's very ill! He's complaining of breathing difficulty! Also, his pulse rate is beating very fast! Can you get a taxi ready for us? I'm bringing him down now."

"Room number, please?"

"Room 164."

"Hold the line, please." Putting the telephone down, the

receptionist gets off her chair and rounds the counter. She takes several steps forward and looks out the front entrance door. She returns to her former spot and lifts the telephone to her ear. "I don't see any taxi waiting at the compound entrance. But there's a trishaw. You want trishaw?"

"Anything, anything!"

"*Becak! Becak!*"

Ah-Chye turns to see a Nepali security guard walking towards him. "Got passengers waiting in the lobby," he says. "Can you bring your *becak* to the entrance?"

"Of course!" Ah-Chye cycles his trishaw to the front porch. His jaw sags when he sees Yuta and Amy coming out of the entrance. *It's them again! Something's wrong with the Japanese man!* Yuta's face is contorted in anguish and one hand is slung over the shoulder of his companion. They take slow steps to Ah-Chye's trishaw.

"Go to Campbell Street," Amy says. "There's a Chinese medical store with a highly reputed *sinseh* [traditional doctor]."

By the time Ah-Chye reaches the medical store thirty minutes later, Yuta's condition has worsened. He slings his arms over the shoulders of Ah-Chye and Amy and shuffles with some effort to the *sinseh*'s consultation room.

Inside, Yuta sits at a desk across from the *sinseh* and Amy manoeuvres his wrist palm-up to rest on a small pillow. Ah-Chye hovers beside Yuta. *Wow, the sinsesh looks like a professor.*

The *sinseh*, who is wearing a goatee and a pair of gold-rimmed spectacles, feels Yuta's pulse. "What's your problem?"

"Breathing difficulty, palpitations and a bloating sensation."

"What did you eat yesterday?"

"Durians."

"How many?"

"Four."

"Did you drink alcohol after that?'

"Yes, brandy and vodka."

"You're very lucky. Alcohol and durians don't mix – the combination could have killed you." The *sinseh* slips the cuff of a blood-pressure monitor over Yuta's upper arm and jabs at a button. The cuff inflates and tightens. Seconds later, it deflates with a hiss and the monitor displays the readings on its screen. "Blood pressure's high." He removes the cuff, casts his gaze down at a writing pad in front of him and starts to write a prescription in Chinese. "Can you boil the herbal medicine yourself? If not, we can boil it for you, but you'll have to wait thirty minutes."

"I'll wait – I'm staying in a hotel." Yuta's voice is a feeble croak.

"Normally, it requires one hour's boiling time but since your condition's serious, we've to cut corners." He tears off the prescription and hands it to a waiting store assistant. "You've to drink the first bowl immediately; then we'll boil another bowl for takeaway back to your hotel. Drink the second bowl six hours later. The store assistant will put an easy chair in the waiting area for you to rest."

An hour later, Ah-Chye stops his trishaw under the front porch of Cosmo Hotel and Yuta, assisted by Amy, clambers out. Ah-

Chye gets off the trishaw, moves to the side of Yuta and pulls the Japanese man's arm over his shoulder. Supported by Amy and Ah-Chye, Yuta lumbers to his room. Inside, they steer Yuta to face the king-sized bed with his back. Ah-Chye eyes bulge in their sockets when he sees the bed. *My God! The headboard has fallen off the bed frame! What did they do?* Ah-Chye and Amy lift Yuta's arms away from their shoulders and the Japanese man tumbles backwards into the bed with a grunt, causing the wooden cross slats of the frame to creak. Ah-Chye hands Amy a plastic bag containing Yuta's herbal medicine and she places it on the side table.

"How much do I owe you?" Amy reaches for her handbag dangling from the crook of her right arm.

"Eighty."

Amy opens her handbag and pays Ah-Chye. "You can keep the change."

"Thank you." Ah-Chye stuffs the money notes in his shirt pocket. "Can I use your toilet, please." He turns and starts to walk away.

"Of course."

Inside the en-suite bathroom, Ah-Chye stands at the toilet bowl and unzips his fly. He casts his gaze down and stoops for a closer look. *Holy cow! Five used condoms in the toilet bowl! They did it five times!*

Images dissolve in my mind as Ah-Chye finishes his story. I pluck a golden gob from the husk of an open durian and cast my gaze at him, sitting beside me. "Is your story about the *jeep-pun-kia*

[Japanese] true?" I bite off a glob of creamy flesh and a sweet-rancid aroma races up my nostrils.

Ah-Chye tosses a fleshless durian seed on the table. "Of course." He licks his fingers. "This *ang haeh* is delicious!"

Ah-Chye and I are eating durians at a stall at Anson Road, which is dotted with shady rain-of-the-forest trees.

"Any more stories to tell me?"

"I've several as I've been a trishaw rider for ten years." He prises another flesh-covered seed from a durian husk with his fingers. "My stories can take up several pages of your book."

Back in my hotel room in Gurney Drive, I search on my laptop for scientific studies on durian as an aphrodisiac. As reported in the *Asian Journal of Biological Sciences*, [Volume 3. No. 1, 2010 edition], Dr. Venkatesh Palaniyappan of the Sir C. R. Reddy College of Pharmaceutical Sciences in Tamil Nadu, India, found that mice fed with durians over a 14-day period had higher sperm counts and higher sperm mobility as compared to a control group not on a durian diet. They also had sex five times more often than the control group. No wonder, there's an Indonesian saying that goes like this: *Saat durian mulai jatuh, sarung malah naik.* [When durians fall, the *sarungs* are lifted up].

* * *

Sucking a toothpick, Ah-Chye exits a coffee shop on Muntri Street, George Town, after his breakfast of toast, soft-boiled eggs and a cup of coffee. The rising sun is peeping over the rooftops of buildings and the drag is almost deserted.

As he moves towards his trishaw parked outside the coffee shop, an African woman, possibly in her mid-twenties, is also taking long strides to his vehicle. "Take me to Stewart Lane, please." Her voice brims with impatience; her English is accented. "Can you be fast? I'm late for an appointment." She is dressed in a short sleeveless dress with a V-shaped neckline.

"Sure!" As the trishaw rolls away, Ah-Chye hears a voice holler, "Stop! She stole my wallet!" He looks over his back to see a fat foreign man with tousled hair, sporting crumpled shorts and a collarless T-shirt running after the trishaw. "She's a thief!" *Possibly a Middle Eastern tourist.* His awkward manner of running makes Ah-Chye look at his feet. *Great Scott! He's wearing hotel room slippers!*

"That's a lie!" shouts the woman. "He said he had insufficient money to pay me; asked me to follow him to the ATM. I checked his wallet and took my due payment." *Sounds like a dispute between a sex worker and her client.*

A minute later, Ah-Chye hears the hoot of another trishaw. Looking behind, his eyes span wider. Pedalled by a scrawny man, the trishaw is chasing him with the large foreigner as passenger.

The woman slaps a palm against the cushioned seat. "Faster, my man! Faster!"

After several moments, Ah-Chye throws another glance over his shoulder, and he gapes. The foreigner and the rider have swapped places. The foreigner is now pedalling the trishaw and the rider has become the passenger. Ah-Chye scowls. The pursuing trishaw is catching up with him. *Dammit! That fatty's a good trishaw rider!*

A short distance ahead, just before the Hainan Temple, the African girl shouts. "Stop! Stop! Stop here!"

Ah-Chye squeezes the brake levers on his handlebars with all his might, bringing the vehicle to a stop. His passenger jumps off. "You sit down! I'll pedal! Quick! Quick!"

Ah-Chye hops into the carriage and sits leaning forward, his heart thumping at the excitement of the flee-and-pursue, and the African girl starts to pedal furiously. As the trishaw approaches an intersection, it swerves to the right to avoid an old man on a bicycle drifting across. "Eeeeeek!" the African woman screams as the vehicle crashes into a monsoon drain. Flung off the saddle, she lands on top of Ah-Chye who is thrown on the pavement a split second earlier. Unhurt, the African woman gets up and starts to run away.

His wind knocked out, Ah-Chye waves his hand frantically. "Hey, my payment!" He slowly gets to his feet. "I want my payment!"

While running, the woman opens her handbag, takes out some notes and throws them on the road. As Ah-Chye goes to pick them up, the second trishaw whizzes past him. At the next intersection, the vehicle and the African woman turn and disappear from sight.

* * *

Sitting in the carriage of his own trishaw parked outside Monaco Inn (not its real name) at Macalister Road, Hussein sees a beefy man and a short man walking out of its entrance. He bolts upright when the two men start to walk towards his trishaw. As they get nearer, he leaps out of the carriage, yanks away a towel hanging around his neck and slaps it against the cushioned seat a few times.

The duo stops a few feet away from Hussein, whose eyes gleam with anticipation.

They are garbed in collarless T-shirts of different colours and casual slacks.

The larger of the two, wearing spectacles, asks, "Can you take us to a karaoke with GROs?" Half-bald, he is probably in his early fifties, has a squat nose and bunched-up eyelids circling his small eyes.

"I know all the naughty places in George Town." Hussein hops aboard the saddle. *They sound like local tourists.* "Come, get in."

"Wait!" the short one snaps. "How much? Where're you taking us?" He has small eyes with brows that almost meet in a straight line and his hair is cut short.

"Burmah Road, sixty ringgit."

Mr. Shorty takes out his smartphone, taps its screen and slides his finger to move the map that has appeared. "Come on," he says, looking down at the screen, "Burmah Road is very near. Thirty ringgit."

"The KTV club is at the far end of Burmah Road, sir. Hussein points in a vague direction. "Forty. I can also wait for you without any charge."

"Okay, then."

The mamasan strides to the VVIP karaoke room of Cheers KTV Club (not its real name), knocks twice on the wooden door and pushes it open. The stink of stale cigarette smoke assaults her nostrils but that does not bother her. She steps in and stands aside to hold the door open for four GROs behind her to enter.

Mr. Beefy and Mr. Shorty are sitting on a sofa and popping salted nuts into their mouths. The babes stand in a line with their backs to one wall and the mamasan moves to the side of the sofa. "Gentlemen, let me introduce my girls!"

Mr. Beefy jerks upright, removes his spectacles and wipes them with a cotton handkerchief. "Only four?" He puts on his spectacles again.

"The rest have still not arrived yet, a few others are putting on make-up." The mamasan looks at her charges. "From left to right: Ngoc from Vietnam, a university student, eighteen years old, first time in Malaysia;" – the pretty girl with a curvy body forms a heart with her hands and smiles – "next is Huong, also Vietnam;" – the plain-looking lanky lass hitches up her skirt to reveal her crotchless silk panties, making Mr. Beefy's spectacles slide down his nose – "third babe is Rachany, a genuine Cambodian jade, speaks a little bit of English, but very playful; and the last girl is Prija" – she blows a kiss at Mr. Shorty who returns the favour – "from the Land of Smiles – she's a former Bangkok car-show model." The mamasan pauses. "All can give bathroom service except Ngoc."

Mr. Shorty waves his hand at Prija who clomps over on wedges to sit beside him. Mr. Beefy sweeps his gaze across the other three girls again. Ngoc locks her gaze with him, puckers her lips and kisses the air. A tingle throbs in Mr. Beefy's loins and his pulse quickens. "I want Ngoc!"

His cheeks flushed, Mr. Beefy takes a gulp of Asahi beer, releases a burp and puts his mug down. Sitting beside him, Ngoc is cracking watermelon seeds between her teeth, looking at the massive LCD monitor in front. Lyrics are running across the LCD monitor but no one is singing.

Mr. Beefy turns to kiss Ngoc on the cheek and there is no reaction. He cups her face with one hand and twists sideways to plant a kiss on her mouth but she turns away. "Darling, no kissing!" She holds his wrist to pull his hand away from her face.

Mr. Beefy casts a glance at Mr. Shorty and Prija, who are snuggled in an armchair diagonally across from him. Her skirt hitched up revealing lacy panties, Prija is straddling Mr. Shorty with both her feet on the armchair. She is kissing him, her tongue twirling in his mouth, and at the same time, Mr. Shorty is squeezing the cheeks of her buttocks with both hands. *Dammit! I should have chosen Prija!* Mr. Beefy exhales a blast of regret.

Now, Mr. Beefy cups one of Ngoc's breasts but the feel of thick fabric padding does not thrill him. He slips his hand under her blouse and starts to slide it upward. The smooth satiny quality of her skin heats up the blood in his groin.

"Darling, no touching!" Ngoc pulls his hand away, folds her arms across her chest and sits up straight, keeping her knees together.

Shit! I've been tricked by her fake friendliness earlier! Mr. Beefy gets up, takes a few unsteady steps forward to the armchair where Mr. Shorty and Prija are locked in an embrace. He taps the shoulder of Mr. Shorty, who opens his startled eyes.

"Ah-Kok, let's swap girls!" Mr. Beefy rubs his hands gleefully.

Prija breaks the kiss and rests her head on Mr. Shorty's chest, her hands clinging to his shoulders.

"Why?" Mr. Shorty's loud voice is hostile.

"My girl's not co-operative."

Mr. Shorty gesticulates with an open palm. "That's your problem!"

"Come on, be a sport!" Sharp furrows bite into Mr. Beefy's brows. "Prija's not your wife!"

"No way!" Mr. Shorty yells, his breath spewing the stink of brandy. "You're soooo ....stupid! You should know that pretty girls seldom deliver good service."

"How dare you call me stupid?" Mr. Beefy hikes his chin, his eyes blazing. "I should shove a beer bottle up your ass!" With a grunt, he grabs the arm of the chair and topples it sideways, spilling Mr. Shorty and Prija on to the carpeted floor.

Mr. Shorty gets up and makes an American-football-style tackle at Mr. Beefy who falls backwards.

"Eeeek!" Prija screams. "Ngoc, get the bouncers!"

The dark-tinted glass doors of Cheers KTV Club swing open and two burly bouncers lead Mr. Beefy and Mr. Shorty out by the back of their shirt collars.

Hussein steps up to one of the bouncers, a man with a pockmarked face, and asks, "What happened?"

"They were fighting!" The bouncer releases Mr. Beefy. "All

because of a GRO!"

Mr. Beefy and Mr. Shorty stagger to the trishaw and climb aboard.

"Back to our hotel," Mr. Beefy says, then compressing his mouth flat in a grim.

Hussein pedals away. Midway to the hotel, he overhears his passengers talking: "Papa, I'm sorry I called you stupid."

"That's alright, Ah-Kok, I shouldn't have lost my temper."

What! A father and his son fighting over a GRO?

* * *

Jeremy, a forty-year-old businessman from Kuala Lumpur, picks up his smartphone from the dresser and taps the screen. He reads the WeChat message he received while he was shaving in the bathroom minutes earlier.

New Car From Laos
Just Arrived Yesterday
New Engine, Low Mileage
Name: Leilana
Age: 19
Price: RM230 (1 hour)
Call Oscar NOW!

An upper-body photo shows a girl with big sparkling eyes under curly lashes, high cheek bones and a straight-edged nose. Her beige T-shirt is stretched tight across her ample breasts. She is at a beach, and her dainty hand is lifted just about to sweep away wind-blown strands of hair covering her mouth. *Not bad looking.*

And it's not easy to get a Laotian girl back in KL.

Jeremy calls the number in the message. "Hello, Oscar? Is your photo of Leilana real?" He cradles his phone between his ear and shoulder.

"Yes, of course, one hundred percent real." The voice is courteous.

Jeremy pulls his pajama trousers down to his knees. "She isn't a ladyboy, is she?" He steps out of them and the blue cotton folds drop in a crumpled pile at his feet.

"Boss, there're very few ladyboys in Laos. I guarantee she's a girl."

Jeremy picks up his bundled pajama trousers and tosses them onto the bed. "Got outcall?" He strides to the closet at one corner and slides its louvered wooden door open.

"Sorry, boss, only incall. Leilana has several appointments lined up. She cannot waste time travelling around."

Jeremy snatches his pair of briefs hanging from a clothes hanger. "Can DFK?"

"Up to her, boss. If you're pleasant looking, smell good, excellent chance of high GFE!"

"Where's your place?" He puts his briefs on.

"Jasmina Hotel, Penang Road. You want to fix an appointment?"

That's nearby. Jeremy clucks his tongue. *Too far to walk but too near for a taxi. A trishaw will be fine.* He takes his trousers, which are draped over the rung of a metal clothes hanger and steps inside them. "Yup, for today." He pulls the zipper and buttons up.

"What time do you want?"

Jeremy holds his mobile phone with his left hand. "Four in the afternoon." His right hand starts to unbutton his pajama shirt.

"Sorry, all afternoon slots have been booked. How about 7 pm?"

Jeremy casts his gaze at his shirts in the closet. "Sure, that'll be fine." He whips a long-sleeved shirt from its hanger.

"Okay, call me when you've arrived."

In the small lobby of Jasmina Hotel (not its real name), Jeremy sinks into a seat on a sofa and scans his surroundings. *Good ... there're CCTV cameras at the reception counter and at the ceiling lines.* He takes out his smartphone and reads several business emails until the appointed time. He then calls Oscar who gives him Leilana's room number.

Minutes later, Jeremy is standing outside her room. He presses the doorbell and, seconds later, the handle is turned downward from the inside. The door swings open inward and his leather heels click as he steps into the room. A girl of about five feet three inches is still holding on to the handle and is about to shut the door.

Jeremy's eyes span wider in shock. *Sweet suffering saints!* His frustration escapes in a bluster of air.

From an oval-shaped face framed by long hair, a pair of lively eyes is staring at him. Her nose is perfect and her deep cleavage promises hidden joys. However, her mouth reveals rotten teeth, which are in various stages of decay. With nary a word, Jeremy braces the door with one hand before it swings shut, yanks it open wider and walks off.

Minutes later in the lobby, when he starts to head to the glass front doors, his mobile phone rings, and he answers it. The ID shows it's from the pimp. "Oscar! Don't take me for a fool! The profile photo does not show her pitiful teeth."

"Mister, that's not the issue." Oscar's voice is cold and hard. "You booked her but never take her? You must pay a penalty! Fifty ringgit! Otherwise, my thugs will be waiting for you outside your hotel!"

"Don't mess around with me. I'm a *lau-jiao* whore-monger." Jeremy's voice is calm and steady. "You don't scare me. You want me to bring the police to this hotel and put you out of business?" He ends the call.

Fifteen minutes later, Jeremy arrives back at his hotel on a trishaw. There's no sign of any thugs waiting for him outside.

* * *

Simon, a solo backpacker from Perth, Australia, steps out of his guesthouse in Love Lane. As he walks towards Chulia Street, which is chock-a-block with bars and budget hostels, he hears the ring of a bicycle bell behind him. Before he can turn to look, a trishaw passes him and stops at the roadside. The trishaw rider, an Indian man in his mid-thirties, gives him a hearty greeting. "Good evening, sir! You want transport?"

"No, thanks!" He notices bouquets of roses sticking in the side grilles of the trishaw and adds, "Nice trishaw, mate."

At Chulia Street, George Town's backpacker haven, he pops

into a 24-hour convenience store to buy a packet of cigarettes. Two women are hanging around on the pavement. As he steps out of the store, one of the women accosts him. "Hello, handsome man!" Her husky voice betrays that she is a transsexual. "Want short time with me?"

Simon ignores her and crosses the road to Hong Kong Bar and takes a table. He was here the previous night and chatted up two female travellers from New Zealand. He had a great time and tonight he's hoping to bump into his new friends again. Luck is with him and he meets them.

Come 2 a.m., the party breaks up. Simon is tipsy, but as a gentleman he escorts his friends back to their inn nearby. When he tries to return to his guesthouse, he's unsure which direction to head to and toddles down a lane. Further ahead, he sees a trishaw parked at the roadside and as he approaches it, he hears muffled groans. The trishaw is also rattling intermittently. A plastic sheet hangs from the hood of the trishaw to the end of its floor. *Huh? What's going on? Usually, the plastic is hung up only when it's raining.*

Simon takes out his mobile phone from his pocket, points at the window in the back of the canvass hood and switches on the torch light. "Hey! Get that light off us!" Simon's jaw drops. *Jesus Christ!* The transsexual who was earlier at the convenience store is having sex with the Indian trishaw man whom he met at Love Lane. *Woohoo! Love Lane's full of love.*

* * *

The mobile on his desk rings and Jimmy picks it up. "Hello, Tropical Island Social Escort." His gaze travels to the computer screen, which is divided into quarters, each small rectangle showing different areas of the lobby. "Ah, Eddy, good to hear from you again. You want to book Yuen-Yuen, the China doll? What time? Hmmm …Yes, she's free. Okay, see you." He ends the call and jabs a number. "Hello? Ah-Ming, any of your old crones speak Mandarin? My regular client's coming at 4 p.m." He releases a chuckle. "Don't get one too old, okay? She must also be slim. You got to brief her on the standard arrangement." He presses the "END" button and calls Yuen-Yuen. "*Xiojie,* you've a special client at 4 p.m. Here's what I want you to do…"

Hours later, Jimmy's phone rings and the caller ID shows it's from Eddy. He scrutinizes the CCTV images on his computer screen and sees Eddy, wearing sunglasses, and the usual trishaw-driver in the lobby. *Nothing suspicious, only two men checking in at the counter.* "Yes, Eddy? Where are you? In the lobby? Great! Give your girl a minute to get ready." *Just to buy some time to re-check the situation. All clear, no cops around.* "You can come up to room 444." Jimmy quickly calls Yuen-Yuen. "Your client's coming up with a friend." In the CCTV images, Jimmy sees the trishaw-driver as on previous occasions leading Eddy by his hand to the lift lobby. The latter is holding a white walking stick.

Clad in a dress ending mid-thigh, twenty-five-year-old Yuen-Yuen goes to the door to open it when she hears the bell. She sees a blind man, possibly early fifties, and another slightly younger man standing in the doorway. The blind man asks his companion something in Hokkien dialect and the latter replies, "*Si, si-he.*" Without uttering a word, Yuen-Yuen steps aside and gestures with an open palm. Nudged from the back by his companion, her john steps inside, tapping his cane on the floor and against one wall. With the driver left outside, Yuen-Yuen closes the door, locks it and leads the blind man by the hand to the chair at the dresser. At that moment, a slim woman crawls out from under the bed. In her late forties, she is the resident cheap prostitute of Ah-Ming's low-class brothel and has seen better days. "*Qīn'ài de* [darling]!" She latches one hand on his wrist. "*Rang wo dainǐ qùxǐshǒujiān* [let take you to the bathroom]! As they move towards the bathroom, Yuen-Yuen crawls under the bed.

"So, by supplying a cheaper sex worker, the *ore kooi thau* [pimp] gets a bigger cut." Ah-Chye wipes his fork and knife with a piece of serviette.

"How do you know there were two women in the room?" I grip a morsel of oyster omelette with my chopsticks.

"Once, after the deed was done, I went to the room to fetch Eddy. To my surprise, I caught a glimpse of another older woman about to come out from the bathroom. She quickly retreated inside." Ah-Chye slices a piece of chicken chop with his knife and fork. "Blind and horny, it's a tough call. He's happy and the Ah-Ming's old hookers continue to earn." He pops the piece of chicken chop into his mouth.

2

Jaunts by Rickshaw

From a cloth bag hanging from the handlebars of his trishaw, Poh-Teik (not his real name) takes out a bottle of water, unscrews the cap and takes a gulp. His trishaw is parked on the roadside outside a hotel under the shadow of a block of high-rise buildings. He replaces the bottle in the bag and returns to his former spot on the pavement that he was sitting on seconds ago.

From across the road, he sees a lanky man coming out of Thye Wan Health Centre next to the Catholic Information Centre. Carrying a bulging canvas briefcase, the lanky man approaches Poh-Teik. A squeaky voice rolls from his thin lips, "What's your charge for an hour?"

"Fifty."

"That's tourist price. I'll pay you twenty-five – I'm a local from Bukit Mertajam."

"Forty. Today's a hot day." Poh-Teik notices that he's wearing cheap canvass shoes and an old watch, probably bought from the flea bazaar in Rope Walk.

"Thirty per hour, I'm going to several places. Take it or leave it."

I doubt he can afford forty so thirty's better than nothing. "Okay, okay. Where to?"

"Take me to a few hanky-panky hotels." The lanky man

climbs aboard.

Poh-Teik pushes the trishaw off its metal stand, swings a leg over the saddle and steps on the pedals. *I see, he's looking for women.* "I'll take you to Waterloo Hotel (not its real name) at Leith Street."

Minutes later, the trishaw rolls past the gateway of the five-storey hotel and stops at the front entrance. The lanky man climbs out. "Please wait for me. I may or may not be long."

"Enjoy yourself, sir." Poh-Teik staves off a smirk on his lips. "I'll park across the road at Red Garden food court. When you're done, I'll come over."

By the time Poh-Teik finishes his Pepsi-Cola, he sees the lanky man standing at the gateway entrance and rides his vehicle over.

"Where to now?"

"Another naughty hotel."

Poh-Teik manoeuvres the rickshaw in the right direction. "The girls here not up to your expectation?"

Not answering his question, the lanky man clambers aboard. "Where're you taking me next?"

Poh-Teik starts to pedal. "I'll take you to Paris Hotel, Irving Road." After a while, he hunches on the handlebar. "Irving Road was named after Charles John Irving, who held a few posts during the British era. He was Acting Lieutenant Governor, then Resident Councillor and finally Auditor-General."

The lanky man remains silent, indicating an obvious lack of interest in history.

Soon, they reach a row of pre-war heritage building and an old fading signboard outside a shophouse says "Paris Hotel" in English and Chinese. The lanky man gets off and disappears inside. Ten minutes later, he re-appears with his face glowing with happiness.

Has he a fetish for older women? He seems happy! "Want to go another hotel?"

"Of course! Of course!" The lanky man hops aboard with more agility than before.

Poh-Teik squares his shoulders and inhales deeply to fortify his energy. "Hock Aun Hotel, Dato Kramat Road – here we come!" His cheeks bloat like those of a puffer fish as he exhales and inhales to the fullest capacity. "This hotel has a gruesome history. A prostitute was murdered by her lover in 2007. He was given the death sentence by hanging."

At Hock Aun Hotel, the lanky man enters and exits in a jiffy with his face in a scowl. "Any more places to take me to?"

"We'll go to Soo Chow Hotel, Kampung Deli Road, near Macalister Lane. The hotel's near a steamboat restaurant." *Wow! This is going to be quite a lucrative ride!* Leaning forward, Poh-Teik pushes his rickshaw to a running start before climbing up the saddle.

Outside Soo Chow Hotel, Poh-Teik takes another glug from his water bottle after his passenger has entered inside. *Strange, why is this man going from one brothel to another?* He dips his hand into his trouser pocket, pulls out a face towel and wipes sweat off his forehead. *Is he suffering from excessive sex drive?*

The lanky man comes back to Poh-Teik's rickshaw after a quick visit to Soo Chow Hotel. "Where else?" He starts to whistle a happy tune.

Poh-Teik scratches the back of his head. *Soo Chow mainly has old whores! Why's he so happy after coming out?* "One final place that I know of is Savoy Hotel, Hutton Road."

The lanky man shows a thumbs-up. "Great!"

When the lanky man comes out of Savoy Hotel, he asks to be taken back to Thye Wan Health Centre on Penang Road. Along the way, Poh-Teik says, "Wow! You're like a stud horse! What's the secret of your virility?"

"What stud horse? I'm a bra salesman! My products are from a multi-level marketing company. I'm checking out new potential markets here. That's why I needed you to show me those hotels. Today, I've secured several lucrative orders, will be back tomorrow to fulfill them." He gets out, pays Poh-Teik and points to a black Proton Wira parked at the roadside outside the health centre. "There! My car's over there. Bye!"

I gesture towards Poh-Teik's half-empty mug of Guinness Stout with an open palm. "*Lai, lai, lim chiew* [Come, come, drink your stout]! You want another bottle?" I spear a piece of *lor bak* [pork spring roll] and pop it into my mouth.

Sitting across from me, Poh-Teik nods and continues to chew his *char kwey teow*.

A waiter weaves his way between the crowded tables and I holler at him, "Guinness Stout, one more bottle!"

Poh-Teik and I are eating lunch in Ho Ping Coffee Shop, located at the junction of Penang Road and Kampung Malabar Lane. His trishaw is parked in a designated stand outside Peking

Hotel housed in a building of Art Deco design.

"So, did you meet the bra salesman again?"

"No, but there was another unforgettable character." He grips a plump prawn with his chop sticks and pops it into his mouth. "A scrawny man who's quite tanned for a Chinese – he was fighting his inner demons."

* * *

Three years ago ...

Eight o'clock in the evening sees Chulia Street bright with neon lights and loud with music blasting from bars and cafes. The pavements are filled with tables taken up by tourists, drunks and local barflies drinking and eating like there's no tomorrow. Rows of stalls set up along the drag sell a cornucopia of local food and the air is filled with both exhaust fumes and an exciting vibe.

His arms and legs crossed, Poh-Teik is leaning against the saddle of his trishaw parked outside a 24-hour convenience store. *One more passenger and I'll call it a night,* he decides as he scans one end of the drag to the other.

Minutes later, a scrawny man appears from the shadows and ambles toward Poh-Teik. "Take me to Victoria Street," he says, his words slurred. Poh-Teik catches a whiff of alcohol and his passenger slumps into the seat of the trishaw and leans back.

Minutes later, Poh-Teik leans forward on the handlebar. "We're in Victoria Street. Where you want to stop?"

"There ...further up ...that biscuit store there."

The trishaw rolls forward for about ten metres and stops. His passenger gets up on unsteady feet and fishes for his wallet to pay him. At that moment, the headlights of a passing car illuminate the scene and Poh-Teik sees that his late-twenties passenger has a wide mouth and a slightly hooked nose.

The next night, Poh-Teik is waiting at the same convenience store, when the scrawny man staggers out of Hong Kong Bar across the road and asks him to send him home. Along the way, the man asks Poh-Teik, "Can you come to my biscuit shop to pick me up at 6 p.m. tomorrow evening? Take me to Hong Kong Bar and send me home so I don't have to drive."

A week passes and, one evening, Poh-Teik plucks up courage to ask, "*Thau-kay*, why are you always drinking? Are you depressed?"

"Yes, I'm depressed."

"Come, tell me your sorrows. Maybe I can give you good advice since I'm older than you." He rings his metal bell to alert a cyclist hogging the road. "What's your name anyway?" He stops pedalling and allows the trishaw to roll on its own momentum.

His passenger releases a loud burp. "Aun-Soon (name changed)."

Poh-Teik applies the brake of his trishaw and stops outside a Chinese coffee shop. "Come, let's stop for a drink." He swings one leg over the saddle and lowers himself to the ground.

Thus begins Aun-Soon's story …

Aun-Soon's seventy-year-old grandpa scans the entries in the debtor's ledger laid in front of him and scowls. He lifts up the fixed-line telephone on the desk and dials a number. "Hello? Hock? Yes, it's me! Come on, your account's sixty days overdue." He releases a blast of frustration. "When can you pay? Hmmm … hmmm …What! From today onwards, its cash on delivery, you hear?" He slams the receiver down, lifts it up again and dials another number. "Michael? Lim here. It's regarding your overdue account. I see …You're nuts!" He bangs the receiver down and storms out of his cubicle into the packing area of the biscuit store where Aun-Soon is inspecting trays of cookies on a long table before they are packed into boxes.

The old man approaches Aun-Soon. "Where's your mother?"

Aun-Soon looks up from the cookies, catching his grandfather's gaze. "Why?"

"I need to tell her off! She granted credit to two clients who're bad paymasters! She should have checked with me."

Aun-Soon's gaze narrows. "Grandpa, it's not entirely Mama's fault. You're always late in writing out the debtor's ledger."

"Why're you siding with that woman?" The old man's eyes gleam like pieces of jagged glass. "She's not even your mother!"

"Huh?" Aun-Soon's eyes span wider in surprise. "What do you mean?"

"Er, nothing." The old man returns to his cubicle.

That evening, Aun-Soon knocks on the door of his parents' room and enters.

His father is leaning on a reclining easy chair and reading a newspaper, while his mother, wearing a long-sleeved flannel nightgown, is sitting in bed and watching a Hokkien movie on a portable DVD player placed atop her raised knees.

His father, togged up in pajamas, looks up from his newspaper. "What is it, son?"

Aun-Soon does not reply and approaches his mother. "I've something to ask you." He sits on the edge of the bed. "Mama, is it true that you're not my biological mother?"

His mother averts his gaze and looks back at the screen of the DVD player. "Who said that?"

"Grandpa blurted it out by accident."

Her eyes gleam with concern from under sparse lashes. "Is that important to you?"

His gaze pleads with hers. "Yes, it is."

Silence, save for the gentle rattle of the air-conditioner, reigns in the room for several seconds before his father says, "I knew this day would come, sooner or later. You better tell him the truth."

His mother presses the "pause" button of the DVD player and puts it away. "Grandpa's right, you were adopted." She draws in a swallow of air as if to fortify herself. "Papa registered you as our baby because we didn't want to go through the hassle of the adoption procedure."

A haze of heat crawls up the back Aun-Soon's neck. "What do you know of my parents?"

"Nothing."

"Any old photos of my mother?"

His mother shakes her head. "No."

"Anyone I can contact to dig into my past?"

"I'll call my friend Choo-Ling (name changed) tomorrow.

Years ago, she put me in touch with the middle-person who was putting you up for adoption. That middle-person's name is, er ..."

"Nancy," Aun-Soon's father chips in. "Nancy Au (name changed) – you're getting old, dear."

"Contact Choo-Ling to get to Nancy, and she may be able to help you." Her voice is stoic. "But bear in mind that Nancy may or may not reveal who your mother is."

"Thank you, Mama. I love you." He tosses his gaze at his father. "And you too, Papa." His voice is flat, as if all emotion has siphoned out.

Two days later in Air Hitam, Aun-Soon manoeuvres his old Proton Iswara outside the gate of the single-storey terrace he's searching for. He gets out of the car and walks to the gate, which is padlocked. A boy of about six is cycling a tricycle in the front compound under a porch. "Is your Papa or Mama in?" asks Aun-Soon, his heart throbbing in his rib cage.

The boy gets off his tricycle and runs inside the house. Seconds later, a woman in her early thirties, wearing an apron and with disheveled hair, comes out. "Yes? Are you looking for anyone?"

"I'm looking for Nancy Au."

"Oh." The woman unlocks the padlock and opens the gate. "Come in."

She leads him to the living room, motions him to a rattan chair and disappears into the back of the house. The little boy reappears with a pear-shaped woman wearing a salt-and-pepper bob. A pair of black cat-eye frame spectacles is perched upon her fleshy nose.

The woman settles into the rattan chair across Aun-Soon. "My daughter-in-law says you wanted to see me?" She pats the boy standing in front of her on the shoulder. "Go, go out and play." The boy patters away.

"Yes, my name's Aun-Soon." He crosses his legs at the ankles.

Nancy blinks and crimps her brows. "Do I know you?"

"Thirty years ago, you were a middleperson in a baby's adoption." A spasm twitters in his jaw muscles. "I was that baby."

Nancy's lips part in surprise. "I was never involved in any such thing. Where did you hear that story from?"

"Madam, it's no use denying it. My mother has revealed to me I was adopted. I also met your friend Choo-Ling yesterday. After lots of persuasion by me, she gave me your last-known address in Jelutong. When I went there, I was told that you had shifted. Luckily, your neighbour, or former neighbour, gave me this address. All I want to know is who my real mother is?"

"I see." A muscle jerks beneath the flabby skin of her throat. "As God is my witness, I don't know where your mother is now."

"Then, please tell me everything you know about her."

Nancy adjusts her spectacles. "Certain things are best left unknown."

"Please …I beg of you."

"You'll not be happy to know of her background."

"That's not important. She's my mother and I need to know."

"Your mother is Thai." She hesitates for a moment as the words struggle to part from her lips. "She was a resident prostitute in Foong Fook Hotel (name changed)."

"What!" Her words produce a rush of heat in Aun-Soon's cheeks. "Where's that?"

His body stiffens like a bamboo pole, and he hears his heart beating in his ears.

"In the old quarter of George Town. Her professional name was Sheila but real name's Nattaporn. I was running the hotel and people referred to me as an *ore kooi poh* [lady pimp]." She folds her arms and lifts her chin to defy the blush in her cheeks. "There were several other prostitutes there as well. One day, your mother told me she was pregnant but didn't want to go for an abortion. She was terribly scared as the last abortion nearly killed her. She asked me to look for someone to adopt her baby when it was born." She unfolds her arms, places both hands on the arms of the chair. "So I spread the word to my friends and Choo-Ling told your mother. Several days after you were born, I brought you to my former place and your parents came to pick you up." Her lips flatten into a stiff smile. "You were a cute baby." The smile dissolves. "A year later, your mother told me she was leaving the profession and was going to work in Singapore. Later when I retired, the hotel was sold, converted into a backpacker's hostel and underwent a name change."

"How old was she when she gave birth to me?"

"In her early thirties. She should be in her sixties today if she's still alive."

"Who's my real father?" Aun-Soon's throat is as dry as Nancy's tone of voice.

"My boy, why are you so naïve? Your father was one of her customers."

"Huh?" Aun-Soon slumps in his chair, shame weighing down his shoulders. "Everything you're telling me now is the truth?" He feels his palms sweating.

"I'm afraid so." A sigh rolls from Nancy's lips. "Porn –that's what I called her – often referred to Hatyai as her hometown so I reckon she was born there. Her husband was a Chinese, and the couple lived in Alor Setar. She was widowed at a young age and came to George Town to work in Foong Fook Hotel. She was there for five years. Your mother's a good woman as she single-handedly fed three kids fathered by her husband." Nancy studies Aun-Soon through sympathetic eyes. "Yes … you look slightly like Porn." Her gaze trails beyond him, out the door to the boy in the front porch. "Sorry, I'm …afraid I've things to do, you've to excuse me."

Sitting across Poh-Teik, Aun-Soon takes a quick swig of his Tiger beer, his Adam's apple dancing a jig, and clonks the frosty stein down on the plastic table. "I'm the bastard son of a prostitute!" The words grind out between his clenched teeth. "Why me? Why me?" He mops a shaky hand over his face. "When I was young, I always felt that my three sisters were favoured over me. Now I know why."

"It's not your fault, is it?" Poh-Teik leans forward and places a comforting hand on Aun Son's shoulder. "Find consolation that you were adopted and given food, shelter and education; there're babies who've been abandoned in garbage dumps and back alleys." His voice is laced with a gentle tone matching the sympathy in his eyes.

"I'm trying very hard to accept who I am." Tears rim Aun-Soon's eyes as self-loathing rises in his throat like sour milk. "Trying to coming to terms with reality." He rises from his chair and takes long strides to the parked trishaw outside, an inferiority complex half-suffocating him.

Back to the present day ...

I lean forward and suck at the straw in my glass of Coca-Cola. "Poor guy, it must have been painful for him."

"I ferried him from the bar to his home for a month." Poh-Teik picks up a piece of *lor bak* with his chopsticks from the plate between us and starts to eat it. "Then Aun-Soon changed his routine. On Monday, Wednesday and Friday, I had to send him to a language school first. He was studying conversational Thai, he told me. One-and-a-half hours later, I'd pick him up from the school and take him to his favourite bar to drink. Two months later, he said he didn't need my service any more as he was going to Thailand." Poh-Teik resumes eating his *char kwey teow*. "I thought that was the last of him, but more than six months later, I suddenly received a call from him. I don't know what Aun-Soon did in Thailand but he had returned to George Town, and had become manager and part-owner of a karaoke bar, which employed mainly Thai GROs. He asked me to go to his bar and pick up a dead-drunk Thai GRO and send her home."

"Is Aun-Soon's bar still open?"

Poh-Teik puts down his pair of chopsticks on the table. "No, it has closed down for more than two years." He lifts his mug in mid-air. "I think it was raided." He sucks a big slurp, leaving a moustache of white foam on his upper lip. "After the bar shut down, Aun-Soon went back to Thailand. That's what his foster family told me." He puts the mug down, pulls out a white cotton face towel from his back trouser pocket and wipes the white foam away. "Curious to know what he was doing there, I called his mobile, but the line was dead."

* * *

Room service waiter Nguyen trundles a trolley along the hotel corridor, his eyes glancing at the numbers to search for the right room. On the trolley are two plates of sirloin steak and two glasses of fruit juices. When he passes a particular room, he hears muffled screaming. He stops, moves to the door and puts his ear against it.

A woman's voice hollers, "Help! Rape! Rape!"

"Gotcha!" roars a man's voice. "You can't escape from me!"

Oh hell! I need to get security! Nguyen runs to the lift lobby, jabs the button and waits. One light panel shows G ...1, 2, 3. Then it stops. *Come on, hurry up! Then* the numerals 4, and 5 appear consecutively and the lift stops again. The other light panel shows G, indicating the second lift is still on the ground floor. Nguyen is on the twelfth floor and impatience takes over. He heads for the fire escape door and pounds down the cement staircase two steps at a time. Gasping for air, he enters the lobby from the fire-escape door. Not wanting to create an alarm, he takes long strides to Devadass, the Nepali security guard hovering near the sliding glass doors at the main entrance.

He taps him on the shoulder. "Devadass, a guest is being raped on the twelfth floor! Come quick, follow me!"

"You sure?"

"Yes, I heard her scream."

Nguyen and Devadass half-run to the lift lobby and find a group of tourists waiting, with both lifts being busy. "Oh hell!" Devadass curses under his breath. "There's a group check-in from a tour bus."

The duo sprint to the fire escape door, and pound up the staircase steps to the twelfth floor. "Which room?"

"There! I left my trolley outside the room!"

Nguyen pushes the trolley to one side and Devadass pounds on the door with his fists. The door swings open a crack with its chain lock still hooked. "Get lost!" a Japanese man hollers. "Go away!"

Devadass takes two steps back and rams the door with his shoulder. He rams again and the bracket holding the chain lock gives way. "Eeeeeeek!" a female voice screams. Devadass and Nguyen dash into the room to see a Chinese girl naked in bed, arms folded over her breasts. An athletic Japanese man, also naked, is standing in a fighting stance next to the bed. His face is a twisted mass of anger.

The Japanese man moves forward to deliver a high kick to Devadass, who parries it with his forearm. Testicles swing from side to side as he follows up with another kick, this time to Nguyen's chest and he makes contact. Nguyen staggers and falls on his back. By now the Chinese girl has grabbed her clothes and bolted for the bathroom.

Devadass dives for his opponent's legs and grabs them, causing him to fall. Now Nguyen and Devadass are over him. They haul him to a sitting position and twist both his arms behind his back. "Xiao Ling!" screams the Japanese. "Explain to them who I am!"

Xiao Ling comes out of the bathroom wearing a halter top and a mini-skirt. "He's my boyfriend!" Her voice is shaky with fright. "We were just role-playing rape. My boyfriend loves BDSM. Release him, please. "

Devadass scrutinizes Xiao Ling with concern in his eyes. "Miss, you're sure you're alright?" He slackens his grip on the Japanese man's wrists. The Japanese man jerks his arms free and rotates his shoulders to make sure they still work. "*Bakero!*" he curses. "I'm going to complain to the manager."

Xiao Ling goes to her boyfriend, who is still sitting on the carpet, and drops to one knee. "Darling, are you alright?" She tosses her gaze at Devadass. "Now please, leave us alone. We've to change rooms because the chain lock is now broken."

My mind travels back to the present as Xiao Ling, a twenty-five-year-old China doll, finishes her story.

"That was my scariest experience here," she says.

Xiao Ling and I are now passing Fort Cornwallis in a trishaw festooned with plastic flowers. Behind us, the trishaw man, Ah-Lum, hollers. "Sir, you want to stop for dinner? There's a food court near the esplanade."

I lean sideways toward Xiao Ling. "You want to eat anything?"

"No thanks, afterwards, I've lots of food to eat at the karaoke bar."

I turn my head and say to Ah-Lum, "Just continue the tour, don't stop."

The trishaw rounds Queen Victoria Memorial Clock Tower, which is bathed in up-lights as dusk is setting in. I recall reading from the Internet that it was built in 1897 to commemorate Queen Victoria's Diamond Jubilee.

I brush strands of fluttering hair from my forehead. "What made you come to Penang?"

Xiao Ling continues her story ...

Singapore
Three months earlier ...
Dressed in a long-sleeved blouse and slacks, Xiao Ling enters the interview room of the Immigration and Checkpoints Authority, Kallang Road, and closes the door behind her.

"Come, please sit down." A bespectacled male officer nods at an empty chair across his desk. He looks smart with his button-down collar and a neck tie, and in his shirt pocket are a black pen and a red pen.

Xiao Ling plops down on the chair, sits upright and rests both hands on her knees. "Good morning, sir." Her hair is tied in a pony tail.

"Good morning, Xiao Ling." The officer looks up from a sheaf of papers in front of him. "A decision has not been made regarding your application for renewal of Student Pass, and a record of this interview will be made, you understand?" He pauses. "Now, in your application form, you stated you've to repeat three subjects because you failed them in your final exams. Why are you confident of passing them in the next exams?"

"I will devote more time to revision and take more notes in class."

The officer scribbles something on a piece of paper and looks up again. "You also did not show up for the final exam on Business Law because of illness. But I don't see any M.C. attached, so what illness?"

Her gut tightens. "Fever. I took my own fever medication, that's why I didn't see a doctor."

"I see." The officer jots down her answer. "Your attendance record shows high absenteeism. Any reason?"

"Period pain every month; sometimes stomach-ache because of eating spicy food. I wanted to cut down on medical expenses, so I didn't see doctor get M.C." *Oh sheesh! Sometimes the hangovers from entertaining guests at the karaoke were as bad as the period pain!*

"Give me the names of your lecturers in Commercial English, Accounting, Principles of Management and Economics."

Oh my goodness, these were the subjects I hated. "Er, Mrs. Lim is lecturer in Commercial English; Suppiah is my teacher in Economics, and …Eric Liew, err, I think it's Siew, not Liew, teaches Principles of Management."

"Who's going to sponsor your repeat studies?"

"Sugar daddy!" Her hand flies to her mouth. *Dammit! What*

a careless slip of tongue. "I mean my daddy back in Wuhan."

Sitting in an LRT train back to her studio-room in Farrer Park, paid for by her sugar daddy, Xiao Ling fishes her mobile phone from her handbag and dials the owner of Foxy Lady Karaoke Club (not its real name). "*Laoban* [boss], I had a difficult interview at the I.C.A. today. My application for an extension of Student Pass is unlikely to be approved. I'll come in for another remaining five more nights, after that I've to pack and fly off." She releases a sigh of frustration. "But I don't want to return to Hubei so quickly. What shall I do?"

"Why don't you go to Malaysia? Either Kuala Lumpur or Penang. There're plenty of karaoke bars and nightclubs there. I'll see you tonight. Bye."

By the time Xiao Ling finishes her story, our trishaw reaches a karaoke bar in Kedah Road. Ah-Lum, the trishaw driver, applies the brakes, which squeal like a cat being tortured. I pull out my wallet and pay Ah-Lum. Then I pay Xiao Ling a tip, as agreed earlier, for her time talking with me. We climb out of the trishaw and Xiao Ling enters the karaoke bar while I saunter to the nearby New World Park to eat Swatow Lane Ice Kacang.

3

Born-Again Devotees

Leaning on stacked pillows, Linda (a pseudonym) is reading a paperback when she hears the unlocking of the front door in the hall. *I better not get up, otherwise I'll feel dizzy again.* She puts the book beside her on the bed and tosses her gaze at the bedroom door, anticipating who it could be. Moments later, the door swings open and in walks her daughter, Susie. She is wearing pixie hair cut that makes her look older than her twenty-eight years.

Susie eases the door shut behind her. "Hello, Mum, how are you feeling?" She pulls the dressing table chair beside the bed and plunks down on it. "Have you taken your medication?" Her voice is edged with concern.

"Of course I have."

"Still having shortness of breath?"

"Yes, if I move about too much."

Susie tosses her gaze at the side table crammed with plastic containers, bottles and a hot water flask. "Everything you need at your bedside?"

Linda turns her head to nod towards a few Tupperware containers. "Yes, Alex prepared my lunch before he left for work." She draws in a feeble inhale. "What brings you here?"

"Mum, I've something important to tell you." Her slit-like eyes fringed with sparse lashes gleam with anxiety. "Please remain calm after I've finished."

"What is it about?"

"Last weekend, while Joe and I were having lunch in Macalister Road, we saw Papa coming out of a hotel across the road." Her gaze turns intense with anger in the depth of her eyes. "He was holding hands with a girl who looks like a Thai. Obviously, he's been up to his neck in hanky-panky during his business trips to Hatyai."

Linda's husband, David (not his real name), runs a wholesaling business in leather products, which are brought in from Hatyai and Songkhla. They are distributed to the northern Malaysian towns, and the deliveries frequently take him overnight away from home.

Heat creeps up Linda's cheeks. "Are you sure?" *Oh my God, looks like my suspicions were right.*

"Of course, Mum, we had a good look at him. Papa and his Thai girlfriend crossed the road and went to the store adjacent to the restaurant we were in."

Leaning back on the pillows, Linda closes her eyes, a silent groan wallowing in her throat, a pain slashing at her heart so hard it's sucking the air from her lungs.

Susie reaches out to cup her mother's hand. "Mum, I want you move out and stay with us. Our maid can look after you while we're at work." Her eyes trail into a sympathetic gaze. "In your current state of health, please don't confront Papa yet. I'll talk to him myself."

The next evening ...

David kicks off his slip-ons, unlocks the front door to his condo and enters the hall. He sees Linda sitting on one end of the couch, watching a movie on TV, her legs stretched out on a round ottoman. As he crosses the hall to go to their bedroom, she flits a cold gaze at him, and then back to the TV. For almost two years, since Linda has been diagnosed with cardiomyopathy, their relationship has been cold with few conversations.

Five minutes later, David comes out of the bedroom in knee-length shorts and a collared T-shirt. His face and body are reeking of the fresh scent of floral soap, and his salt-and-pepper damp hair is neatly plastered to his skull. He settles at the far end of the couch and turns to face his wife. "Where's Alex?"

Her gaze focuses on the TV. "Gone for a movie."

David gives his throat a gruff clear. "Linda, you're a devout Buddhist, aren't you?" He pauses for emphasis. "And in Buddhism, donating one's organ accrues good merits to the donor, isn't it?" *I hope this religious approach with the old cow works.*

Eyes spanned in surprise, Linda takes her legs off the ottoman and shifts to face her husband. "What're you getting at?" Her tone of voice is thick with wariness.

"Linda, can I ask a favour from you?" His right hand dips into the side pocket of his shorts. "I've the consent forms for donation of your kidneys should something happen to you in the near future. The recipient is for a specific person who's suffering from kidney disease." He unfolds two pieces of paper stapled together and holds them in his hands. "You and she have the same blood type so there's a possibility you can be a compatible donor. I need your signature on the forms." He reaches out to hand her the forms.

She takes the papers and looks down at them. "She? Who's she?" She casts her gaze through half-lidded eyes back at her husband.

"A business associate of mine, a Thai girl from Hatyai." The tone of his voice is pregnant with forced casualness. "Her kidney disease may progressively worsen and –"

"Is she the girl you were with at that Macalister Road hotel?"

"Huh? How did you know?" David's muscles stiffen in shock. "Never mind, why yes, she came from Hatyai to consult a specialist at a private hospital regarding her condition."

"Business associate, huh?" Her body starts to quiver with anger. "Don't you dare take me for a fool! You want me to donate my kidneys to that bitch?" Her voice almost cracks with strain. "No!" Short blasts of air roll from her lips. "No way! My God, don't you have any conscience?"

"Come on, Linda, the recipient waiting list at Hatyai hospital is long." He scrunches his face, as if tasted something bitter. "Do you know your heart disease is getting worse day by day? That's what the doctor told me confidentially. Even if you decide to go for surgery later on, there's only a 50:50 chance of success. Why take your kidneys to your grave with you?"

Linda's eyes gleam like jagged glass. "She can drop dead for all I care!" She tears the organ-donation forms into pieces and scatters them on the floor.

"You just threw away a golden opportunity to go to heaven!" His words are as hard as the muscles twitching in his face. "You're a selfish old bitch! Damn you!"

Linda flinches at the sting of his words, her eyes widening in shock, and the next moment, her head and torso collapse to one side.

David darts to the bedroom to get his handphone and calls his son's number. "Alex, come back immediately! Your mum has fainted. I'm going to call an ambulance now."

As David stands waiting in the corridor outside the hospital room, the smell of antiseptic claws into his nasal passages. Moments later, the door swings inward and Alex comes out.

David steps towards his son. "How's your Mom?" His tone of voice is emotionless.

"She has regained consciousness, Papa." Alex sears his father with an accusing glare. "Is it true what Mom said about you?" He folds his arms across his chest. "That you asked her to donate her kidneys to your Thai girlfriend?"

David hikes his chin and his cold gaze meets his son's. "Come on, Alex, the old lady's going to die soon, anyway –" he raises a forefinger and crooks it "– it's just a matter of time. So, why let good kidneys go to waste? I'll be marrying my Thai girlfriend in the near future, you hear?" A flicker in his jaw betrays his effort to control his temper.

At that moment, before Alex can reply, Susie and her husband step out of Linda's room and take short strides to join her brother. "Papa, what you did was totally unforgiveable! Mama almost died from a heart attack triggered by hurt!" She shoots him a cold glare. "I wish you burn in Hell!"

Shock fuses David to the spot at the hatred in her daughter's words. "Shuddup!" He wags a stiff finger at her. "I raised you and gave you an education! So mind your own business!" His hand rises to slap her daughter.

In a blur of movement, Alex throws a blow to his father's jaw, who staggers backward. Face winching in pain, David lunges at his son but his son-in-law steps in between the two men, pushing them apart with his palms pressed to their chests.

A matronly nurse walking past hollers, "Stop it! Both of you!"

The fat, balding bartender of Happy Elephant KTV in Hatyai recognizes David as he steps up to the bar. "*Sawadeekrup*, David, what you want tonight?" He fills up a mug with draught beer and slides it to a waiting bargirl. *Poor guy, he has lost Pensri for good.*

David rakes his fingers through his sparse hair. "I'm looking for Pensri." He stands with feet apart and rests both hands on the bar.

"I'm sorry, Pensri resigned two weeks ago." *Oh Lord Buddha, what he did to his wife is now the gossip of everybody here.*

"Any idea where she is now?"

The bartender shakes his head and his jowls wobble. "I don't know; she packed her things and left suddenly – didn't even say goodbye to me."*It's best to mind my own business as instructed by Mummy.* "Forget Pensri, David, we've two new girls tonight." He thrusts his jaw toward a table to his right. "They're sitting over here. You interested?"

Lips flattened in a straight line, David fumbles in his trouser pocket and takes out his wallet. "Here's my contact." He slips out a name card and hands it to the bartender. "Can you please call me if you know her whereabouts? Or maybe her new handphone number? I've something very important to discuss with her."

The bartender takes the card and puts it in front of him on the counter. "If you're so eager to get in touch with her, why don't you go to her parents' house? They live in Pichit village, just a few miles north." *Poor bastard, he won't find her there as she's gone to Phuket.* His gaze darts in a certain direction. "There, there's Mummy! She should be able to give you the home address of Pensri's parents."

David's eyes gleam with hope. "Thank you." As he moves away and strides towards the mamasan, the bartender's pudgy fingers pick up his name card and tosses it in the waste bin behind him.

Almost a year passes ...

Standing on the pavement outside Diamond Plaza Hotel on Nipat Uthid Road 3, Hatyai, David sees two women strutting down the middle of the drag. They are carrying a horizontal banner with the words "Hatyai Vegetarian Festival". Behind them, three dancers in Chinese lion costumes prance about to the clash of cymbals and the staccato beat of drums. Trailing behind are vans with loudspeakers and white-garbed men carrying fluttering flags and pennants on bamboo poles. A man throws a string of firecrackers on the road and lights it. They explode like the chatter of a machine gun, littering the road with red confetti. When the explosions stop, a voice from a loudspeaker shouts, "*Huat ah!*"

A single row of entranced mediums start to stride past David, whose gaze suddenly sharpens. *It's her!* His breath stills in his lungs; heat burns his cheeks. Pensri is among the mediums. She is wearing baggy white pants matched with a white tunic and a yellow vest with dragon motifs is strapped across her upper torso. Apart from a skewer pieced through both her cheeks, two small skewers are dangling from her ear lobes. Her right hand is raised shoulder-high, thumb holding down the middle finger, the other three fingers extended.

"Pensri!" Jostling past other onlookers, David forges forward to his former lover, the beat of his heart pulsing in his ears. "Pensri, it's me, David!" When he is several feet away from her, he reaches out his hands. "Pensri, let's talk afterward!" Still striding, Pensri tosses a glassy gaze through half-lidded eyes at him for a moment and looks away. Several attendants encircling Pensri block David from advancing any further and hustle him back to the pavement.

Back to the present ...

Pensri grabs a bunch of noodles with a pair of chopsticks and places them in her mouth. "When David came back to my hotel on that day," she says with her mouth full, "his jaw was swollen, and he had suffered a dislodged tooth." She starts to chew the noodles. "When he told me what happened, I became upset and confused because what he did was terribly wrong. I did not ask him to ask his wife for her kidneys, it was entirely his idea."

Pensri and I are sitting in a vegetarian stall outside the gate entrance of the Tow Boo Kong Temple in Lintang Macallum 2, George Town. The afternoon sun sparkles off the ruby stone on her ring finger. Ah-Lum, the trishaw rider, who arranged the meeting with Pensri has parked his vehicle a short distance away under a tree outside the Pelangi Flats, and he has gone to pray in the temple. The Nine Emperor Gods Festival featuring a nine-day-long vegetarian diet is in full swing. Devotees have turned up in hordes to pray and hawker stalls along the roadside are doing brisk trade.

I lean forward to sip my barley drink. "But don't you think his intention was for your good?"

Not answering my question, Pensri looks away and, after several seconds, tosses her gaze back at me. "Three days after that incident, his wife died, presumably of a second heart attack. I felt guilty and got depressed. That got me thinking about the dark side of David's character, and it scared me." She puts her chopsticks down on the table and her tongue wipes sauce from her upper lip. "Finally, I decided to leave him, resigned from the Hatyai nightclub and went to Phuket. Before I left, I called him in Penang, gave him my reason for wanting to end our relationship." She pauses, lifts her glass of Chinese tea and swallows a mouthful. "At first, he cried, begged me not to leave him, but finally, he got angry and shouted obscenities. The revelation of the ugly side of him shocked me." She holds the plastic glass with both hands and twirls it. "Later, I barred calls to my hand-phone from all his numbers." She clunks the plastic glass down. "Two months later, I returned to Hatyai and joined a different bar." Looking down at her plate, she continues to eat and then casts her gaze at me. "It was during that time that I met another suitor, who, coincidentally, is also from Penang. I married him a year later. So, that's how I ended up here; it's been four years already."

I spear a vegetarian fish ball. "Did you recognize David while you were a medium during the procession?" Bringing the fish ball to my mouth, I bite off a piece.

"Yes, but I couldn't control my physical movements. When the procession ended at Wat Chue Chang, I came out of my trance and quickly slipped away."

"How many times have you participated in the vegetarian festival?"

"Once in Hatyai; two previous years here in Penang. Tomorrow night's the fire-walking ceremony, and I'll be taking part in it. So, tomorrow will mark my fourth time." Her eyes brim with contrition. "I've seen the light, and want to earn good merit. That's why religion is important to me now."

"How're your kidneys?"

"One year after my diagnosis, I got a transplant from a donor who died in an accident. By good fortune, the donor's blood type was compatible with mine, not with several other patients who were placed earlier on the waiting list. As a token of gratitude to the powers above, I became a *ma song* [medium] at the Hatyai vegetarian festival."

* * *

Masseuse "No. 16", togged up in knee-length shorts and a collarless T-shirt, slaps Stanley's back with both palms, producing *piak! piak! piak!* sounds which reverberate in the small cubicle. He feels gusts of air knocked out of his lungs with each smack.

Wow! She knows her stuff! Cool air from air-con vents in the ceiling blasts down on his bare upper body, causing goose bumps to rise on his chest and arms.

Five minutes later, he turns over as instructed by the masseuse. She moves to the top end of the massage table and massages his head. Now, she leans forward, causing her bosom to press against Stanley's face. *Ziggety-damn! They're big!* Stanley gulps silently and feels a tingle in his groin under the thick cotton towel. She rubs her open palms in forward-and-backside sliding motions across his chest and stomach. Stanley takes an inhale. *Her perfume's nice!*

The chest massage is over in a jiffy, and she steps to the side of the massage table. "*Laoban*, do you work around here?" She starts to knead his upper arm.

Stanley turns his head sideways to gaze at her. "No, I'm from Taiping." *She appears prettier today with her hair tied in a ponytail as compared to last week with hair in a bun.*

She stops for a moment and adjusts a bra strap. "Where's Taiping?" She jerks her neckline back in place and continues the massage.

"A quiet town about one-and-a-half hour's drive away. It's south on the mainland. What about you? Which part of Vietnam are you from?"

"Loc Ninh, about three hours from Chi Minh City." She starts to squeeze his lower arm. "What brings you to Penang?"

"Part business, part pleasure." *Looks like she and I are getting acquainted. Great!* "I run a trading business. I've clients in Penang."

"May I know your name?"

"Sure, Stanley. What's yours?"

"Duyen." She flicks her gaze at him. ""Last week, you were quiet, hardly spoke. Any problems?" A gentle smile lifts the corners of her mouth. "I'm a good listener, *Sitanli*."

"I was thinking about my youngest son." *She seems to be a caring person.* "I'm a bit concerned about him. He's not getting good grades in college ..."

Forty minutes later, the chit-chat and massage end. "I remember last week you said no happy ending provided." Stanley eyes are filled with lust and hope. "But how about this time?"

"Sorry, *laoban*, this is family-massage centre." The tone of her voice is honey-sweet.

Taiping, Perak
Two weeks later ...

Stanley picks up his buzzing mobile phone lying on his office desk. The caller ID shows Patrick, his friend living in Gelugor, Penang. He rises from his chair and steps out of his partitioned cubicle so that his female clerk sitting a few feet away won't be able to eavesdrop. "Yes, Patrick?" He casts his gaze at his three Bangladeshi workers packing knitted cotton gloves into boxes, but he sees Duyen in his mind's eyes.

"Hello? Stanley, I went to the health centre as instructed by you. I specifically asked for massage lady number sixteen. After the massage, I asked for sex from her. She said no." A pause. "I'm much younger than you, and she still rejected me, so I think she's clean."

"I see, thanks for the feedback." *She's a decent woman, not a cheap whore. Time to ask her out for a date!* "What do you think of her? Pretty?"

"Of course, she's pretty, you lucky man! Best of luck! And thanks for sponsoring the massage."

Three months later ...

Ai-Ling, a property agent, walks down the corridor and stops outside a solid nyatoh wood door. "Here we are." She turns and casts a glance at Stanley and his companion, a Vietnamese woman. *She's quite pretty and the man's old enough to be her father.* She slips the key inside the lock, turns it and pushes the door inside.

Stepping inside the hall, Ai-Ling announces, "The hall has a ceiling fan and there's also a landline telephone." She points to a telephone sitting on the floor in a corner. "There's no arrear in the phone bill."

Stanley goes to the telephone, squats down, lifts up the receiver and dials a number. Moments later, his mobile phone rings. Not bothering to answer his own call, he replaces the receiver back in its cradle. His companion goes to the aluminum glass louvred window and opens it. "*Sitanli*, the views are good." Wind blows in her face, fluttering stray strands of hair against her neck.

Ai-Ling moves to the master bedroom. "The owner left his air-con, which is quite new." Stanley and his companion pop their heads in the doorway but do not enter the room. As Ai-Ling starts to move towards the second room, from the corner of her eye, she sees Stanley putting one hand on the woman's buttocks and squeezing one side. *Holy cow! This man is both impatient and lecherous!* She over-hears him say in a half-whisper to his lover, "That room can take a king bed. When I'm in Penang, I can stay overnight." Ai-Ling flings the door open to the second room. *Looks like the old bastard wants to set up a love nest for his lover and himself.* "This room's smaller, ideal as a study or store-room."

Stanley gives the small room a glance and moves to peek into the bathroom, which has a shower booth. The trio proceeds to the bare dining area. "This space is big enough to fit a square dining table for four people," says Ai-Ling, who then leads the way to the kitchen. "See how lucky you are? There's even an electric oven – model is new – and a hood above." She goes to one wall, taps on a switch and the oven hood hums like an angel's breath. "The oven hood works, of course!"

"Duyen," Stanley says, a tease hovering on his lips, "when I'm here, you can cook for me."

"Just tell me what your favourite dishes are, *Sitanli*." Tender care radiates from Duyen's eyes. "I love to cook, but you've to wash the dishes." The corners her lips upturn in a tease and her voice brims with jest.

Ai-Ling turns on the tap in the sink and water gushes out in torrents. "Water pressure's excellent!" She tosses her gaze at her client. "So, Mr. Stanley, do you want to take this apartment?"

Her client looks at his sex-kitten companion. "I'm fine with this unit, but what about you?"

The Vietnamese woman nods and offers a sunny smile.

Months later ...

From Taiping, Stanley dials the fixed-line telephone number in Duyen's apartment.

"Hello?" It's Duyen's voice.

"*Bao pei*, how was your day?" Stanley's ears perk when he hears something in the background.

"Business was a bit slack. *Qingren*, I miss you. When're you coming up?"

Of course, she misses me. Her monthly allowance is due end of next week. "Next Monday." His gut cramps and he takes an inhale. "*Bao pei*, why is there faint English music in the background?"

"*Qingren*, the TV is switched on."

"*Bao pei*, are you alone in your apartment?" *Odd, during the five months I've known her, she has never shown any interest in English songs.*

"Of course, I'm alone. What do you mean by that question?"

"Nothing, I'll see you next week then. Bye-bye." *Maybe, she has a boyfriend and he's listening to the English songs. Two weeks ago, there was some funny noise in the background, too.*

Half-choking on exhaust fumes, Ah-Ho, a trishaw rider by profession, eases the throttle of his Honda Cub and it slows to a halt outside Bedford Inn (not its real name). He sees Duyen and her male companion get down from their motorbike under the street lamps. They remove their helmets and enter the hotel entrance, a huge bright rectangle with automatic sliding doors. *Odd, why didn't they do it in Duyen's apartment? Why rent a hotel room?* Ah-Ho parks his motorcycle on its side stand on the roadside, keeps his helmet in its front carrier and steps up to the pavement.

Three days earlier, he met Stanley in a coffee shop and was instructed to keep a twelve-hour night surveillance on Duyen and a price was agreed. Tonight is his second night's surveillance. Minutes ago, he saw her coming out from her apartment block and getting on a motorcycle ridden by a man. Ah-Ho bolted to his own motorbike and trailed them.

Presently, upon stepping in the lobby, Ah-Ho sees a few chairs and tables but Duyen and her male companion are not around. A receptionist sitting behind a counter is engrossed in staring at a computer screen. He sinks into a chair, crosses his legs and waits. Within not more than two minutes, the lift glides down and the twin doors slide open. Ah-Ho jerks his head backward in surprise, his eyes bulging in their sockets, when he sees Duyen's male companion step out and go to the sitting area to take a seat near him. *This bugger looks like a Vietnamese.* Epiphany strikes Ah-Ho, causing his breath to hitch in his throat. *There's only one explanation for this situation! This bastard is pimping for her!*

Ah-Ho steps outside to the pavement and calls Stanley. He tells Stanley everything. Stanley ends the call but calls Ah-Ho again after a minute.

"Hey, Ah-Ho! Stop your bloody game with me! I just called Duyen on the landline phone in her apartment and she answered my call!"

"*Thaukay* [Boss], I'm not lying! I can take a photo of her coming out of the hotel entrance if you want me to." Gesticulating with one hand, Ah-Ho ponders for a moment. "*Thaukay*, you've under-estimated your lover. She has set up a call-forwarding facility from her apartment's fixed-line phone to her handphone."

"Dammit! Why didn't I think of that?" A blast of air rolls from his lips. "Go ahead, take as many photos as possible. I'll see you on Wednesday, same coffee shop."

I'm sitting in Ah-Ho's stationary trishaw parked at the esplanade and Ah-Ho is standing across me. In the horizon, the setting sun is painting the sky crimson yellow, and the sea breeze is cool on my face. Ah-Ho takes a long drag of his cigarette. "That Stanley was not fully convinced and wanted to catch Duyen red-handed. So, after his last visit to her, he didn't go back to Taiping, but put up in a hotel in George Town." Ah-Ho exhales smoke through his nostrils. "I continued my surveillance and, the next night, trailed her to another hotel. I immediately phoned Stanley, who drove there. You should have seen the look on her face when she came down and saw Stanley waiting in the lobby." He gives a sad shake of his head. "Now, Stanley is a changed man, having lost some money. He goes for Buddhist meditation classes to find peace of mind."

* * *

November

Joseph (not his real name), aged twenty-eight, pulls the steering wheel of his car over to the left to stop at the roadside outside a Thai Buddhist temple in George Town. His mother is sitting beside him in the passenger seat, her lips clamped in a straight line. They get out of the car and walk under a lighted archway emblazoned with Thai scripts to enter the compound. Cool evening air feathers their faces and twinkling stars above stare down at them.

Minutes later, they find Abbot Bhuridatta seated in his usual corner in the prayer hall, which contains a massive statue of the Sitting Buddha. Wearing a saffron robe, which exposes one shoulder, the monk is sitting cross-legged on a plaited mat laid on a raised dais. Joseph and his mother kneel in front of the monk, place their palms flat together and bow. Next, they place their hands on floor and lower their heads to the floor. Two days earlier, they came to see him, and tonight, there's no need to explain anything.

Abbot Bhuridatta gets up from his lotus position. "Follow me, we'll do the ritual in the room. It's important not to be disturbed." As he steps down from the dais, his gaze travels to the old woman. "You can either wait here or join us inside to observe the ritual." He steps to a bell hanging from a wooden stand, rings it three times and starts to stride toward the back entrance of the hall.

The old lady trails behind his son. "I'd like to observe the ritual."

The trio enters an adjoining room about half the size of a tennis court. Statues of Buddhist deities are standing on an altar placed against one wall. Abbot Bhuridatta lights incense joss sticks and plants them in the urns sitting on the altar. By now, five other monks have entered the room, and one of them has a ball of thick yellow string in his right hand.

"Joseph, join us in forming a circle." Abbot Bhuridatta casts his gaze at the old lady. "Madam, you can sit in the far corner." He looks back at Joseph. "Sit on the floor with your legs crossed, your palms in prayer position."

Once the seven people have sat down in a circle, a monk loops one end of the yellow string around his left palm and passes the ball of yellow string clockwise to the next person who repeats the process. Finally, the ball ends up again with the first monk who holds it between his two palms pressed together.

"Joseph, empty your mind as we recite the *kata,*" Abbot Bhuridatta says, his tone authoritative. "If you feel you're going in a trance, don't fight it, go with it."

Abbot Bhuridatta kicks off the ritual by uttering:

"Wipadti badtikhaahaaya

Sappa sambpadti sittivaa, sappa dhukkha winaasaaya, aadtaanadtiya suttang

Pruudta Mangkalang ..."

After a moment's silence, all the monks chant a mantra in Thai language in tight unison, creating a hauntingly eerie sound, which echoes in the hall:

"Cak hawci khxng phracea nab rxy ...Chan khx khwam chwyhelux xyang temthi

Pldplxy chan cak khwam chaw ay laea wethmntr sida ..."

An hour later, when the ritual ends, Joseph's forehead is damp with beads of sweat. The party troop out of the room. When Joseph crosses the main prayer hall to leave, he slips some money into the donation box placed in front of the Sitting Buddha.

"Thank you," Abbot Bhuridatta says. "We'll repeat the ritual until you're cured."

Late October, a month earlier ...

The movie ends and Joseph, dressed in pajamas, clicks the remote to switch the TV off. Rising from the armchair, he goes to one wall to tap off the lights in the hall and climbs the staircase to his bedroom. Inside, he switches on the air-con and flops on his bed. He shut his eyes and pulls a blanket over his legs.

As he waits for sleep to envelop him, his thought drifts to Regina. In his mind's eye, he sees her oval face in front of him, her long hair cascading over her shoulders, her cherry-red lips pouting, her piggy eyes gleaming with a come-hither look. He pushes her out of his thoughts, flips his pillow over and turns to his side. *Dammit, why am I thinking of her?* Joseph focuses on his breathing and starts to count mentally. *One ... two ... three ... four ...five ...* After the numeral five, three thoughts mushroom in his mind, sputtering his counting to a halt: *I miss Regina, I want to see Regina, I want Regina!*

Releasing a silent groan, he props himself on one elbow, turns sideway to switch off the table lamp. He fluffs up his pillow, lies down again and imagines he's in a cavern filled with darkness, silence and void. Time passes slowly but sleep is elusive. Like a dream, an image of a naked Regina flashes before his mind. His hand reaches to pull his pillow from under his head. Fire licks at his crotch as he swallows the pillow in a hug and wraps his legs around it. *Jesus Christ! I'm getting an erection! Sheesh!* He throws the pillow to the floor.

Taking in a deep inhale, Joseph turns to switch on the side lamp and gets out of bed. He looks at the alarm clock on the side table. Its luminous hands show two-thirty in the morning. He goes downstairs to the hall and wanders aimlessly. *Maybe I should call Regina, talk to her for a while? Sigh, but I'm sure she's asleep by now.* Faced with no other choice, he goes upstairs to his mother's room and knocks on the door.

Moments later, he hears the click of the lock and the door opens a crack. His mother's face – eyes squinting, lips in a scowl – appears in the gap. "What's the matter, son?" Her voice sounds like the crow of an old rooster.

"Mum, I ...er, need another sleeping pill."

"What?" The old lady's eyes span wider, making their crow's feet more prominent. "This is the third time in two weeks." She takes a step sideways and taps the light switch on a wall. "Come inside, Joseph, tell me what's the problem?" Concern is etched in her murky eyes.

Joseph feels the heat from his mother's glare, drops his gaze to the floor, his lips pressed in a straight line.

September, almost two months earlier ...

Joseph rings the doorbell to Regina's apartment and waits. The door swings open and she appears standing in the doorway, a smile curving on her lips to expose slightly crooked teeth. A V-neckline tight top is straining against her breasts that thrust out six inches in front of her! Joseph's gaze trails to her cleavage, and heat rings his collar and his pulse quickens. An equally tight skirt compresses her butt, and her long shapely legs end in a pair of furry house slippers. Joseph catches a whiff of ylang ylang from her perfume and the heat on his collar fires up to his neck.

He steps inside, sinks to one knee to untie the laces of his shoes and slips them off. Regina picks up his footwear and places them on a rack standing near the doorway. "Come Joseph, the food is on the dinner table." A warm gaze from her piggy eyes fuses with his for a second. "Thanks for accepting my home dinner date." She sashays towards the dining table to the right of the hall with Joseph following behind. "How about a beer? Or perhaps a soft drink?" She lifts up a mesh-net food cover from the table to reveal four dishes: *sambal petai* prawn, fried pomfret, steamed white tofu and stir-fried water convolvulus.

"Sure, beer will be fine." Joseph drags out a chair and settles down. "Smells good!" A smile curves his lips. "When's your next trip back to Bentong?"

"Maybe during Mooncake Festival." Regina goes to a fridge standing against a wall and takes out a can of Tiger beer. She pops the lid off the can and deposits it in front of him. "I'll go scoop rice from the kitchen," she says, disappearing into the adjoining room. She re-appears with two plates of rice in both hands and serves one to Joseph. They start to eat and chit-chat.

Partway through the meal, Joseph asks, "Why aren't you eating the *sambal petai* prawn?" He swallows the food in his mouth and takes a swig of beer.

"I've a sore throat – you go ahead and finish the dish." Her tone of voice is light but her expression is heavy.

August

Suhu [Sifu] Peng, a practitioner of Taoist black magic and also a fortune-teller, flicks his gaze up to the wall clock for the second time. His client, Regina, is late for her appointment. Holding a Chinese brush in one hand, he casts his gaze down again and continues to write Chinese characters on a strip of green paper, eight inches in length and three inches in width. As he scribbles, his lips chant a strange mantra in Hokkien dialect.

Ten minutes later, Regina is sitting in front of *Suhu* Peng across his desk. She places her tote bag on her lap, takes out a small plastic bag – its open end tied with a rubber band – and hands it over to him. "*Suhu*, this bag contains my sanitary pad."

Suhu Peng takes the plastic bag, takes a deep inhale and holds his breath. He unties the rubber band, opens the bag and looks inside. "*Wah* …such a copious discharge! Excellent! This is what I need." He re-seals the plastic bag with the same rubber band. "I'll need three days to prepare the charm." His gaze darts to a calendar on a wall. "So, you need to come back next Monday."

"I've another request." Regina pulls out another plastic bag from her tote bag. "My makeup set is going to finish soon. I need a fresh set. Can it be done by next Monday as well?"

"Sure." *Suhu* Peng stretches out his hand to take the bag.

Three days later, *Suhu* Peng hands Regina a small bottle filled with murky liquid. "Cook something to feed your man, preferably a dish with gravy. During the cooking, add three tablespoonfuls of the liquid to the food. If it doesn't work the first time, do it again. I'm confident that after the third time, the magic will be potent."

Holding the bottle in front of her, Regina squishes her eyebrows in curiosity. "What's this inside?"

"Water and the ashes of a paper love talisman." He pauses for deeper impact. "Plus the power of three nights' chanting of mantras." He pauses again. "It also contains your menstrual blood!" The tone of his voice is as deadpan as the look in his eyes.

"Huh?" Regina's slit-like eyes jolt wider. "Yucks! Ewww!" She sticks out her tongue in disgust. "Err, shall I avoid eating the charmed food?"

Suhu Peng jerks open a top drawer. "Of course, definitely!" He takes out a small transparent plastic bag containing lipstick, lip gloss, foundation and powder. "Here're your cosmetics." He passes the plastic bag over to Regina. "Charmed, sealed, and delivered!" A chortle rolls from his lips as he laughs at his own joke. "For maximum effect, use them liberally."

July

Joseph clicks "Shut down" on his computer screen. *Thank God it's Friday!* He picks up his mobile phone and calls his buddy. "Hello? Kiat? I'm going drinking tonight, any place you care to recommend?" He pauses. "Yup, I was in Latino Heat last week, great place with lots of lookers, but that club's pricey. Any cheaper places?" He pauses again and presses a button on his computer screen. "Mainland? No problem." He picks up a pen. "Golden Sands KTV, Perai." He scribbles on a piece of paper. "Sungei Wang Sports Bar, Times Nightclub, both in Bukit Mertajam." He scribbles again. "Any naughty places in Icon City? Hmmm …hmmm …I see. Thanks, Kiat." He picks up his briefcase and clocks out of his office.

An hour later, Joseph is sitting in a dim space with a brightly lighted wall at the far end where there's a shiny bar. At one end, dozens of glasses are stacked pyramid-style, and a beer barrel occupies another end. Joseph leans forward on his settee and takes a sip of his Smirnoff vodka. Around him, tables are taken up with men and their hostesses, and saxy jazz music is seeping from hidden speakers. He leans back and drums his fingers on the arm of the settee impatiently.

Twenty minutes later, the mamasan – her wrists and fingers wearing gold – strides to his table with a twenty-something girl in tow. "*Thaukay*, sorry to keep you waiting." A smile hovers at the edges of the mamasan's mouth. "We operate under the butterfly system and all my girls were engaged." She casts a quick gaze at her lassie. "May I present our most popular hostess, an *ang pai* [red number]!"

The hostess's crimson lips open like red rose petals blown apart. "Hello, darling, my name's Regina!" With a sway of her hips, she slinks to the empty seat beside Joseph.

Joseph feels heat braising his cheeks, and his breath hitches in his lungs. *Wow! She has more curves than the Japanese Grand Prix circuit and is probably twice as dangerous!*

Back to the present …

Joseph and I walk out of the Kuan Yin Teng Temple at Masjid Kapitan Keling Road after praying inside. The front compound is crammed with stalls at the perimeter, and we step to a bird seller to each buy a small cage containing two birds. Today is the first day of the Chinese lunar month and smoke swirling from burning giant joss sticks in the compound is smarting my eyes.

We move to the centre of the compound and I lift my cage aloft with one hand. "How many times did you undergo the ritual?" My other hand opens the small door and the two birds flit away.

"Three, and they cured me of the *kong thau* [black magic]." Joseph scrutinizes his birds from up-close. "They're cute, huh?" He tosses his gaze at me, with the cage held in both his hands. "Actually, Regina's only got a hot figure but her face is not pretty." He utters a silent prayer and continues, "So, I was surprised with myself that I was giving her three-figure tips at the bar and falling for her." He opens the door of the cage and sets the birds free. "When I confessed to my mum that Regina's a bargirl, her hunch was that I was a victim of black magic. So, she took me to undergo the *suad pan yaks* ritual." His gaze follows the direction of the birds as they soar upward. "I'm now a more religious person. I pray at temples more often."

We stride back to the bird seller to return the empty cages to him.

* * *

Joe, a Malay trishaw rider in his late thirties, and I are queuing at a street stall called Nasi Kandar Imigresen at Market Lane, George Town. As we shuffle along, I tell him to go sit in Asia Café after he gets his food. Soon, the Mamak hawker passes each of us a plate of rice and we load them with chicken kurma, curried squid and *begedil* [fried potato patty]. I pay the hawker and Joe and I take a table in Asia Café, a fan-ventilated coffee shop.

"*Teh tarik ais,*" Joe says to the waiter and he goes to wash his hands at the sink.

"Barley *peng.*" I wipe my fork and spoon with a piece of Kleenex tissue.

Joe returns to his seat across from me and wipes his hand with a serviette plucked from a plastic packet.

The same waiter brings our drinks and I pay him. "So, what's this incredible story you want to tell me?" I ask Joe as I shovel a spoonful of gravy-soaked rice to my mouth.

"It's about this taxi driver." Joe starts to eat with his right hand. "His name's Waliyudeen."

Ten minutes ago, I met Joe (that's how introduced himself) at the shady pavement of Buckingham Road outside Masjid Kapitan Kelang. My hail-fellow-well-met manner won him over for a chit-chat about the escapades of johns he has encountered. He accepted my invitation for nasi kandar lunch, so, I hopped onto his trishaw and he took me to Market Lane, near the Sri Mahamarriam Temple.

Now, as Joe relates his story I mentally squint into the past ...

Sitting in his taxi, Waliyudeen leans back and focuses on Passion Nightclub (not its real name) tucked in a building in front of him. He flicks a glance at his watch. *Almost 1 a.m. Should have drunken customers who can't drive leaving soon.* Minutes later, two men stagger out and move to the first taxi in the queue and Waliyudeen starts his taxi to move his vehicle a spot up. He's now second in line. Much later, a group of three men stroll to the first taxi and get in. *Great! The next customer's mine!* Minutes later, Waliyudeen jerks upright in his seat when a woman garbed in pants and a short-sleeved floral print blouse ambles with rubbery knees in his direction. She's carrying a shopper bag in the crook of her right arm.

The woman grabs the handle of the back door, yanks it open and climbs in. "Take me to Jelutong Road, Danaka Apartments."

She's an Indonesian. Waliyudeen starts the engine and pulls out of the taxi rank. He casts his gaze at the rear view mirror. *Quite a young girl. An oval-shaped face with pouting lips. Shoulders are quite big, possibly did manual work when she was young. Fuyoh! She's also got big breasts!* The toot of a car behind prompts him to look ahead at the road. *Ooops! I've encroached on the other lane.* He steers his taxi back to its proper lane.

After a while, he hears vomiting and looks at the rear view mirror again. His passenger is bent over and spewing stale whisky on the floor. "I'm so sorry …" She lets out a groan. "I've also stained the cushion. Send your car for cleaning, give me the receipt and I'll reimburse you." She tugs out a piece of tissue from her shopper bag and wipes her mouth.

Waliyudeen screens down his window to let the stink of stale liquor run out. Later, he scans the buildings on both sides of the road. "We're at Jelutong Road. Where's your apartment?"

"Further ahead, take second left after Public Bank."

A minute later, Waliyudeen pulls the taxi over to the side of the road. "We've arrived."

The woman sits upright and takes deep breaths. "How much

do I owe you?"

She grips her temples with her thumb and forefinger and massages them for a while.

"Twenty ringgit." *Sheesh! Her breath stinks!*

As she fumbles in her shopper bag, she suddenly presses a hand to her mouth to suppress another rising retch. "Ugh ...I still feel dizzy."

"Why don't you pay me tomorrow? I'll be at Passion Nightclub. "

"That's sweet of you." The woman opens the door, swings her feet on the ground and gets out. After closing the door, she takes several steps forward and her knees buckle, causing her to end up on all fours. Her shopper bag falls to the ground, spilling out its contents: a small leather purse, stiletto heels, a mini skirt, a mobile phone and a halter top.

Waliyudeen gets out of the taxi and takes quick long strides towards her. "Let me help you." He slides both arms under her armpits and hoists her to her feet. Then he stoops to gather her belongings, tosses them into her shopper bag and returns it to her. "I'll walk you to the ground floor lobby, just in case you fall again." They take slow steps to the compound entrance and a security guard steps out of his wooden shack. "Visitor? Please register." His gaze travels to the woman. "Good evening, Miss."

The woman turns to Waliyudeen. "I'll be alright. No need to inconvenience yourself. Good-night." She waves and staggers away.

Waliyudeen tunnels his hand inside his trouser pocket to take out his wallet. He fishes out a folded piece of paper. "Here, the cost of cleaning my taxi." He unfolds the paper and hands it to Vivi who places it lying flat on the table.

Vivi opens her handbag, takes out some money and hands it over. "That includes your taxi fare. Please keep your change."

A Bangladeshi waiter appears at their table. "Roti Hong Kong?" The waiter lifts up a plate filled with bread topped with an egg wrapped around a hot dog.

Waliyudeen jerks his chin in the direction of Vivi. "For her."

"Roti Abu?" The dish resembles *murtabak* and is topped with mayonnaise and raisins.

"Mine."

"Milo Dinosaur?" The waiter holds a tall glass aloft.

"Over here," Vivi says.

Finally, the waiter sets a glass of Horlicks Dinosaur in front of Waliyudeen and goes away. "Please pay at the counter afterward."

Earlier, when Vivi climbed into Waliyudeen's taxi, he invited her to supper at Restoran KSB Cahaya at Macalister Lane. On the way, they made a joke of last night's incident and formally introduced themselves.

Waliyudeen stirs his drink. "Do you have valid travel documents?"

"Of course. I've a work permit as a *pembantu rumah* [maid]." Vivi starts to slice her bread with a knife and fork. "But I ran away after six months. My ex-employer ill-treated me."

"What were you doing in Indonesia?"

"I was a kitchen helper in a small restaurant in Medan."

"Are you single or married?" *I hope not! I hope not!*

"Single."

"Divorced?"

"No, never married. I'm only twenty-three, still young." Her eyes sparkle under long thick lashes. "What about you?" She spears a piece of bread and pops it into her mouth.

"Divorced." *I hope this lie will give me an upper hand in my pursuit of her!* "I'm thirty-eight this year. My children are with my ex-wife."

Four months later ...

Vivi opens the front passenger door of the taxi and climbs aboard. Her facial features are downturned, and her mouth is scrunched in a scowl.

Waliyudeen turns his head sideways to face her. "What's wrong, darling? You look unhappy."

"Mount Sinabung has erupted." Her voice wavers, as if on the threshold of an onslaught of tears. "My ...my family's house in Tiga Pancur village has been destroyed."

"Are they alright?"

"Luckily, they managed to escape. But they're now homeless." From her shopper bag she takes out a folded copy of *Berita Harian*, a Malay language newspaper, dated 22nd May, 2016. "My father needs at least sixty million rupiahs to rebuild the house." She unfolds the newspaper, turns to a certain page and shows it to Waliyudeen.

Waliyudeen's fingers switch on the dome lights and he reads the news. "I'm so sorry."

"Please send me home. I've no mood to eat supper." She blinks several times and a sheen of tear invades her eyes. "Darling, I'm very worried for my parents."

"Err, is there a way I can help?"

Vivi takes out her handphone, jabs "speaker mode" and dials a number. After a few ringtones, she says, "Hello? *Ayah* [Father]?"

"Yes, Vivi, why're you calling at such a late hour?"

"I'm with my boyfriend Waliyudeen. We're discussing how we can help to rebuild your house."

"*Sayang* [darling], say hello to my father, Basuki."

"Err, how do you do, sir."

"*Saudara* Waliyudeen, my daughter has spoken so much about you. Thank you for sending her home safely every night." Puffs of laboured breathing accompany every few words he speaks. "I'm glad that she's found a good man, and I'll be more than happy to have you as a future son-in-law once I get over this difficult patch."

"Thanks for the kind words, sir. May I know where do you live?"

"I live in Tiga Pancur village, but I'm now in a relief centre because my house has been buried under volcanic ash." A noisy sigh of sadness rolls from his chest and he coughs a few times. "I can't sleep every night because the air is choked with sulphuric smell, which aggravates my asthma."

"*Ayah*, you get some rest, okay?"

"It's been nice talking with you, *Saudara* Waliyudeen. *Selamat malam* [Good night]."

Vivi ends the call and replaces her mobile into her shopper bag. "It's up to you, darling." She shifts in her seat, digs out a tissue from her shopper bag and wipes her eyes. "I don't like to ask money from you, darling" – her tongue stalls from words she seem reluctant to say – "but if you can help my father out, I'll be most grateful."

Waliyudeen ponders for a moment. "I can sell this taxi. I finished the hire-purchase payments several months ago."

A week later ...

"I'm looking for Vivi," says a man with a flat face.

The mamasan of Passion Nightclub squishes her eyebrows in puzzlement. "Vivi has gone back to Indonesia." *He doesn't look like any of our customers.* "Who're you?"

"I'm a close friend." Mr. Flat-face's eyes become round with shock. "When did she go back?"

"Three days ago."

His lower lip trembles. "She has gone back to Medan?"

"No, she's not from Sumatra." *Oh dear, she has told him a few lies.* "She's from Jakarta. I know because when she applied for a job here, I asked her to show me her passport, and I saw a Jakarta address. On her last day, her boyfriend came to fetch her on a motorbike. Odd, on that day, she used the back door and left early. I've spoken to her boyfriend before as he used to send and fetch Vivi from work during her first week here. If I'm not mistaken, his name's Basuki."

"*Puki mak!* I've been conned!" Mr. Flat-face spews the words out like they were poison. "My taxi ...my taxi ...gone forever ..." he mutters to himself as he walks off with eyes in a daze.

My mind jolts back to the present as Joe finishes his tale. I finish eating my nasi kandar and push my empty plate away. "How could that taxi driver be so stupid? He was talking with Basuki who was right here in Penang, and he never suspected that? I can't believe it!" A chuckle erupts from my lips.

"As they say, love is blind." Joe takes a sip of his *teh tarik ais*. "And Basuki sounded old over the phone."

"How do you know?"

"My real name's Waliyudeen and that taxi driver is me." His eyes brim with remorse as he scrubs his palm over his face. "Now I come to Masjid Kapitan Keling to pray every day." He squares his shoulders as if to shake off the hurt he suffered. "I want to atone for my sins because I was nasty to my wife when I was involved with Vivi."

4

Happy-Ending Massage

Seated in the spectator stand of the Penang Turf Club, Thomas Tan (a pseudonym) peers through his binoculars as he watches the horses gallop towards the final straight. As he squints, his ears are focused on the commentator's voice blasting from an overhead speaker:

"They're now in the last two hundred metres! Leading is Tokyo Girl, behind by half a neck is Jimbaran. Running on the outside one length behind in third place is Silver. Holy cow! Silver now shoots forward like a bullet! It overtakes Jimbaran! Now, Silver and Tokyo Girl are racing neck to neck! Ooooh ...Silver wins by a nose!"

Thomas Tan, a professional illegal bookie, curses under his breath. *Damn! Double damn! The payout is twenty for Win and fifteen for Place.* He replaces his binoculars in their case, takes out a packet of cigarettes and lights one to calm his nerves. After taking two puffs, he sees three punters who earlier placed winning bets moving towards him.

"Thomas!" says the first punter, flapping his palm face-up. "Today's my lucky day!"

Thomas wipes sweat off his brows with his sleeve and digs into his trouser pocket for his thick wallet.

That same evening ...

Thomas glugs a mouthful of beer and leans forward to plant a kiss on the rosy cheek of his GRO, who's wedged between him and the arm of the settee, but before his lips make contact, his mobile phone buzzes.

The GRO takes his mug of beer away and places it on the coffee table, setting his hand free to fish out his mobile phone from his belt pouch. "Hello?" Thomas says.

"Hiyaah! Ah-Loong here! I've struck first prize in today's Dai Mai Cai! Winning number of 3458."

"Huh?" Thomas sputters. "How much did you bet?" *Dammit!*

"Thirty ringgit" The voice brims with delight. "So, when can I collect my winnings?"

"Come on Monday, please." Thomas' eyes gaze trail into a distant stare. *Hell! Another punter also bet heavily on that same number!*

His GRO slaps his lap. "*Qing ai*, anything wrong?"

Three days later:

Inside the prayer hall of a temple in Paya Terubong, an attendant is beating a camphor prayer block with a small wooden mallet to produce rhythmic *tok! tok! tok!*, while another man is chanting prayers. They are standing beside a wooden table where a medium is seated facing statues of The Goddess of Mercy, who is flanked by the God of War and the Monkey God. Standing on the other side of the prayer table is Thomas and his eyes are almost watering from swirling smoke from joss sticks in an urn. A minute later, the medium rolls his head in circles and his open palms slap the table repeatedly. Then, with a cry that sounds like the hoot of a gibbon, the medium springs up backward. He lands with both feet on the seat of the chair, raises one knee and one hand scratches at his right ribs. "*Tai Seng Yah* [Monkey God] is cordially invited here!" the prayer-block beater says, the tone of his voice respectful. The medium leaps off the chair, adorned with dragon carvings, and sits down.

Thomas leans forward toward the medium. "*Tai Seng Yah*, my name's Thomas Tan, I need your assistance."

"What's your problem?" asks the Monkey God through the medium, whose legs are shaking like the tail of a rattlesnake.

"*Tai Seng Yah*, my luck's very bad. I'm a professional bookie, and this month I've lost heavily. Can you please help me?"

"What's your birth-date? And time?" He scratches the back of his head.

Thomas gives him the information.

The medium counts using his thumb and fingers. "Based on your *pay-ji*, you shouldn't be experiencing any bad luck during this period. That's from the viewpoint of astrology. But a source of ill luck has affected you. So, recently, did you attend any funeral? Or visited a columbarium? Or someone in the maternity ward of a hospital?"

"Nope."

"How about a house of pleasure?"

"Er, I went to a massage parlour." Thomas gives a feeble clear of his throat. "A masseuse massaged my back using her feet! Then, err ..."

"*Tsk, tsk, tsk!*" The medium slaps the table with one open

palm. "That's where the source of the bad luck came from!" His upper lip curls backward like that of a chimpanzee's. "The massage lady was having her menstrual period!" He turns to his attendants. "Talisman!" The prayer-block beater places a yellow strip of paper about two inches wide and six inches long on the table in front of the medium and hands him a brush. As the medium gazes down to scribble some Chinese characters on the talisman, he instructs Thomas, "Buy seven types of flowers, put them in a pail of water, burn the talisman in a container and pour the ashes in the water. Give yourself a good cleansing." He hands the talisman to Thomas. "Make sure water flows from your head to the toes, understand?"

Thomas takes the talisman with both hands with reverence. "Thank you, thank you!" He steps away from the table.

"Next!" The prayer-block beater hollers.

* * *

"Darling, I'm going for supper at the night market," Ken says, stepping out of his pajama trousers, "and a cold beer. Are you joining me?" He starts to wear his casual slacks and T-shirt. "I'd also like to take a browse."

"You go ahead," says his wife. "My back's sore. I think I'll just watch TV."

Later, Ken is traipsing down a narrow walkway running the length of the Batu Ferringhi Night Market. He stops at Long Beach Food Court and eats grilled seafood and sloshes it down with Tsingtao beer. As he weaves his way through the crowds back to his hotel, a tanned woman, who looks like somebody's grandmother, accosts him, "Aromatherapy massage, sir?" She hands him a flyer, which gives the various prices and the location of the spa in a nearby hotel. "Only five minutes' walk away. I can bring you there."

He looks up from the flyer. "Prices are expensive. But what nationality are the girls?"

"Iban, Kadazan, from East Malaysia, got Indonesians – all young girls."

Ken moves a step closer to the female tout and lowers his voice. "Can I have happy ending?" His eyes twinkle with hope; his crotch pulses with desire.

"Of course! You've to negotiate with the girls directly."

Ten minutes later, Ken is lying face up on a massage table and a petite Kadazan lass is slathering his arms with oil. *Pooey! This is not aromatherapy oil! More like baby oil scented with something! This is not a good start.* She pinches his arms with her thumbs and forefingers. *Sheesh! Her technique's poor!*

"Massage harder, please." He blasts out a gust of frustration. "No, still not hard enough." The masseuse does not reply but continues as before for another two minutes.

Ken lifts his head up and turns to look at her. "Today, I drove for almost seven hours from Singapore to get here, do you understand? My arms are really tired, so can you squeeze harder."

The masseuse steps away from the massage table, collects her basket containing her towels and aromatherapy oil and starts to walk away.

"Where're you going?"

"Please wait, I'll be back." Her icy tone is matched an icy glare from her eyes as she casts a backward glance at him.

A minute later, the door of the massage room swings opens and in steps a massage lady old enough to be Ken's mother. He gasps in horror and bile rises to his throat. *Holy smoke! She's also the size of a gorilla!*

"Let's continue with the massage, boss." Her voice sounds like the rumble of a tractor's engine.

"Ouch!" Ken squirms in pain as his biceps are caught in pincer-like grips.

"Not so hard!"

The masseuse moves to one thigh and executes what looks like a professional wrestling clawhold. Ken almost flops on the massage table. "Arrrrrgh! Softer, softer, please."

The painful squeezing and kneading continue intermittently for another thirty minutes before the massage ends.

The next morning, Ken goes to take a shower before he changes to go down for breakfast. As he steps naked out of the bathroom, his wife gets out of bed.

Her gaze sweeps from his upper torso to his legs. "What did you do yesterday evening?" Her lips curl in displeasure.

"What do you mean?"

"Go take a look at yourself in the mirror."

Ken steps to face the dressing table mirror and his eyes become rounder from shock! His limbs and body are covered with bluish bruises.

* * *

The car Herlina is travelling in stops at a double-story house in Gelugor, Penang.

Sitting beside her is her agent who yanks the handbrake up and kills the ignition switch. She picks up her cell phone from the centre arm-rest and calls a number. "Mrs. Ang, your maid has arrived. We're outside your house." She ends the call and turns her head towards Herlina. "Come, take your suitcase – your employer is a good woman."

Minutes later, Herlina, aged thirty, is introduced to Mrs. Ang, a broad forty-something woman with a stern look about her, and the agent takes her leave. The next morning, under Mrs. Ang's supervision, Herlina has prepared a pot of coffee, six soft-boiled eggs and several slices of toast. As she is setting them on the dining table, Mrs. Ang goes to the foot of the staircase and hollers, "Ah-Keong! Come down! Breakfast's ready!" She goes back to the dining room and says to Herlina, "Take the Kraft cheese out of the fridge and the *kaya* as well. Then you can rinse the vegetables in the sink."

Herlina hears the couple's son come bounding down the staircase. Then there is the screeching of chairs as Mrs. Ang and the young man seat themselves at the dining table and start to eat. Moments later, Herlina hears the thud of a walking stick as Mr. Ang, referred to as Ah-Keong by his wife, takes slow steps down the staircase. Yesterday, she saw him once but they never spoke. She hears an "Ow!" and the sound of him falling with clumsy clonks on the wooden steps. Rushing to the foot of the staircase, she sees Ah-Keong sprawled across several steps midway, his face grimacing in pain.

"Mr. Ang, let me help you." She starts to move to the staircase.

"No! Leave him alone! Let him get up by himself!"

"Yes, madam." *I wonder why? Their son is also not bothered! Strange ...*

When breakfast over, the trio leaves in a Toyota Alphard driven by Mrs. Ang.

One weekend afternoon, Mrs. Ang goes to her neighbour's house to play mahjong. While Mr. Ang is slouched on the sofa, watching the ASTRO channel on TV, Herlina is mopping the living room floor. As she works around the sofa, she stops and asks, "Mr. Ang, I know it's none of my business, but why is your wife not treating you nicely?"

Mr. Ang tosses his gaze at her. "So you noticed?" He lowers the volume of the TV using the remote control. "When I was fit, I treated her well. Now that I'm handicapped, I am subject to abuse. Is that fair?" He gestures to an empty seat across the coffee table. Sit down, let me tell you my story ..."

In a massage centre in George Town:

"Come, turn over," the China-doll masseuse says. "Now, I'll work on your back. Just relax your spine."

Eager to ask for happy ending at the end of the massage, Mr. Ang flips his skinny body over, the corners of his rubbery lips upturned in a grin. He tucks his face in the breathing hole of the table.

The masseuse picks up a cotton towel and drapes it across his back. She pushes a plastic stool to the edge of the massage table, hitches her skirt higher and kicks off her sandals. She climbs on top the stool and transfers her feet to the separate edges of the massage table, her legs straddling Mr. Ang. Gingerly, she plants one bare foot on his shoulder, then the other foot.

"Ooooh ..." Mr. Ang grunts.

"Am I too heavy?"

"Nope, just perfect." Mr. Ang chortles. "I've had heavier woman on top of me before!"

The masseuse starts to walk in small steps on his shoulders. "*Suan mah* [Is it nice]?" Then she proceeds downward to his upper back and moves to the lower back. She lifts herself on the balls of her feet and starts to walk on the spot.

"Ooooh ...nice ..."

"Eeeeeeek!" One of the masseuse's foot slips! *Smack!* She falls and lands crotch first with legs straddled on Mr. Ang's lower back.

"Arrrrrrgh!" Mr. Ang's face contorts in pain.

The masseuse gets off Mr. Ang and returns to the floor. "Oh, I'm so sorry!" She pulls the hem of her skirt down. "Are you alright?" She helps to turn him over. "I lost my balance."

"My goodness! My legs feel numb!" He starts to massage his own thighs. "I can't move my legs!" He almost breaks into a sob. "My spine's injured!"

"What to do now?" The masseuse's face turns pale.

"Get my handphone! It's in my right trouser pocket. I'll call my friend to help me to a hospital."

An hour later, Mr. Ang is lying on a hospital bed.

"Ah-Keong, what happened?" Mrs. Ang is standing at his bedside. "Did you play your regular tennis?"

"Yes, I was playing tennis with Anthony when I fell backward." Mr. Ang puts on a poker face with much effort. "I tried to get up but could not. He and another club member sent me here in my car." He slaps his thigh with one hand. "Now, my legs are still numb, and I've difficulty moving them." He draws in a noisy breath. "An MRI has been done; now, I'll have to wait for the report. Let's hope for the best."

Mrs. Ang rubs her right palm over his arms. "What's this? Why're there traces of oil on your arms?" She slips her hand under his white tunic and glides her palm over his chest. "Your body's oily too! In the name of hell, you were in a massage parlour! And something went wrong during the massage, isn't it?"

Ending his story, Mr. Ang runs one hand over his face and latches his gaze to Herlina's with moist eyes. "I was confined to a wheelchair for more than six months. After months of therapy, I've regained partial use of my legs."

"Oh, you poor man!" Herlina's eyes brim with sympathy. "It was such an unfortunate accident."

Their gazes fuse for several moments.

"Err, Herlina, do you know *pijat* [massage]?"

She cocks her head sideways. "Why?"

"I haven't had a massage for a year." His lips twist into a grin filled with lust. "Since we're alone, can you *pijat* for me? I'll pay you."

Herlina's jaw drops.

I put down my bamboo chopsticks and push my empty plate with the dregs of flat noodles away. "So, did that bookie cleanse away his bad luck?" I slide my glass of iced Pepsi-Cola towards me and take a sip.

"Yes, he was on a winning streak again after going to the temple," says Ah-Chye, sitting across me.

Ah-Chye and I are eating *char kwey teow* in Hock Ban Hin Cafe at the junction of Siam Road and Anson Road. Earlier, we ate durians at Anson Road and he recommended that we eat *char kwey teow* from the famous mobile stall, which stops outside the café at 3 p.m. Ziggety-damn, he's right – the *char kwey teow* is good.

"Back to Herlina, did she give in to Ang's advances?"

"She did, but Ang's already impotent," says Ah-Chye as he flicks his gaze at me, "so strictly it's only massage."

* * *

"Now, roll over and put your face in the breathing hole," Diep says. "I'm going to massage your back." She kicks off her slippers, takes a folded towel from a nearby table and snaps it open.

Aloysius, a young spa newbie, flips over, snuggles his face in the breathing hole and hangs his hands over the edges of the massage table. "No, not like this." Diep lifts his arms up and places them on the massage table. She spreads the cotton towel over Aloysius' back, raises one foot on the massage table and, with one hand, pushes herself up to a standing position. "Relax, relax your back." She walks gingerly on Aloysius' back and, midway into the massage, coughs with vehemence. "*Hack! Hack! Hack!* Sorry, too much smoking." Aloysius ignores her, having been soothed by the dim lights, cool air and slow music from her handphone.

Earlier, Aloysius, a sales manager from Kuala Lumpur, paid for a package, which included happy ending. Then the pimp hollered "Lineup!" and ten girls of various nationalities trooped out from the back. They stood in a line in front of Aloysius and he chose Diep because of her big assets. *Wow! They must measure at least 36 inches!*

Now the massage is over. Diep climbs down, undresses and tosses her clothes in a pile on a table in a corner. Aloysius sits on the massage table and his manhood shrivels. *WTF! She's flat-chested! I've been cheated by a push-up bra! Might as well get this over with quickly. Dammit!*

He tosses a glance at the door. "Aren't you going to lock the door?"

"Doors cannot be locked during a massage." Lying on the massage table, Diep stretches her open arms to receive him. "This is City Hall regulations. Come, darling."

After the happy-ending deed, Diep showers him, towels him dry and leaves the cubicle. Aloysius takes his pants from a clothes hook behind the door and steps into them. He dips his hand inside his trouser pocket and feels his wallet. *It's still here, and still as thick as before.* He dresses up and leaves for dinner.

Later, at Gurney Drive Hawker Centre, Aloysius orders

cuttlefish with convolvulus for dinner. He fishes out his wallet, pulls out a money note and hands it over to the apron-clad hawker.

"*Kan ni na [Damn you]*!" The hawker flings the money note in Aloysius's face. "Why you give me a piece of Hell Bank note?"The money note flutters to the floor.

Aloysius's jaw drops. Eyes widened in shock, he pulls out a stack of notes in his wallet. *Jesus Christ! My money's been stolen and replaced with Hell Bank notes!*

Back in the spa, Diep up-ends a bottle of Singer Sewing Machine Oil to drip oil into the hinges of the door in the cubicle that Aloysius was in earlier. *The loot just now is lucrative! Luckily, I coughed to mask the creaking of the hinges!* Her conspirator, a petite Vietnamese girl who sneaked in to steal Aloysius' cash, swings the door a few times. "There's no noise now. We better oil the doors in the other cubicles as well."

5

Gigolo Escapades

Wyatt Wong (a pseudonym) steps up to the glass doors of Eight Seasons Hotel (not its real name) in Perai, and they slide open automatically. Cool air caresses his face as he scans the lobby, which is empty except for a receptionist at the front desk.

He jabs buttons on his mobile phone and starts to walk towards a chair. "Hello? Zoey? I'm Wyatt." He plops down on the chair. "I'm in the lobby now."

"Can you go to the coffee house?"

"Sure. I'm wearing dark pants and blue shirt."

Inside the coffee house, he grabs a table near the entrance so that his client can see him easily. A few minutes later, a woman, possibly early thirties, enters, spots him and makes making a beeline for his table. She has on a brown pencil skirt and a matching sienna jacket pulled over a beige blouse. *Today's my lucky day! A slim young woman!*

"Hello, Wyatt." Zoey extends her hand and her teeth gleams white against her tanned skin. "You look exactly like your photo."

Wyatt stands up and pumps her hand. "How do you do?" A smile nudges the edges of his lips. "Err, my payment first, if you don't mind." *Oh shucks! I'm willing to do it free!*

A waitress hands them a laminated single-page menu each.

"No problem, but not here, later in my room." Zoey looks at

the menu. "Can we get a drink first?" She turns her head sideways to look at the waitress. "Caffee Americano."

"Caramel Latte."

They return the menus to the waitress who goes away.

Wyatt leans forward, places both arms on the table and clasps his hands loosely. "Are you from Penang?"

"I'm your client. " Zoey hikes her chin. "I ask the questions, okay?" A wry smile plays on her lips. "Where do you work?"

"Why, of course." Wyatt harrumphs. "Hawaii Fitness, George Town branch – it's part of an international chain."

"Yes, I see you're physically fit."

"What's your blood group?"

"Huh?" Wyatt blinks and raises his eyebrows. "My blood group?" *What's she getting get?*

"Come on, that's no big secret, isn't it?"

"Blood type is A positive."

The waitress brings them their hot beverages.

"Attended university?"

"Nope, but I spent two years in a college."

Zoey takes a small sip of her Caffee Americano. "Parents still alive?"

"Father has died, mom's still alive." Wyatt lifts his cup in a mocking toast, swallows a gulp, then sets it down.

"What illness?"

"Heart disease." Wyatt scrunches his brows. "Err, why all these questions?"

"Just trying to know you better." She lifts her cup again for another sip and eyes him over its rim. "Got girlfriend?"

"No, I don't want to get committed at too young an age."

She takes a deep swallow. "You visit prostitutes?"

"What!" Wyatt's heart almost stalls in his chest. "What kind of question is that?" He pauses for a second. "Err, sometimes, but I've always practised safe sex."

"What's your astrological sign?"

"Leo."

"Good! Leos are ambitious." Zoey downs the rest of her coffee. "Can we go to my room so we can talk in private?" She waves one hand at the waitress and makes a scribbling motion with her thumb and forefinger held together.

Inside her room, Zoey goes to lower herself in one of two chairs at the coffee table and Wyatt settles in the other chair. "Here's your escorting fee." She opens her handbag, takes out some money notes and hands them over.

After Wyatt has slipped the money into his wallet, she continues, "Let me get straight to the point – I want your sexual services without condom."

"Holy cow! No way!" Shock curdles in Wyatt's throat. "I'm not taking any risks!"

"Please, hear me out first before you decide." Zoey opens a paper bag lying on the coffee table and takes out two small cardboard packages. Each measures about 6 x 4 inches. "These are HIV self-test kits. We'll each do an HIV blood test now." She holds one package aloft. "Since HIV has an incubation period, we'll do another test one month later." She thrusts the package to Wyatt. "Then we can have raw sex on our next appointment."

Wyatt reaches out to take the kit. "Where did you get this?" He reads the front side of the box.

"I bought it online."

Wyatt flips to the back of the package. "I see, it's made in Japan ... Hmmm ... antigen and antibody test ...for faster detection ." He looks at Zoey. "Why're you going through all this trouble?"

"Sex is always more pleasurable without condom."

"If you get pregnant, that's not my problem, okay?" He puts the package on the coffee table. "And I won't pay a single sen for child maintenance."

"Of course! I'll be on contraceptives."

"But this HIV testing was not mentioned during your booking. So I reckon a surcharge will be in order."

"Surcharge? Call it whatever you want, but my tip is an additional fifty."

Wyatt considers for a moment. "Okay, deal!"

Zoey picks up a box, opens it and spills out an aluminium-foil package. She tears the package open and pours out a lancet, an alcohol swab in a sealed wrapper, a strip of paper, a micro pipette, a folded instruction leaflet and a small bottle of buffer solution. She picks up out the pamphlet and reads it. "Come, sit next to me," she says, and Wyatt shifts his chair closer to her.

Zoey strips away the wrapper of the test strip and places it on the table. "Your forefinger, please." She tears open the wrapper of the alcohol swab.

Leaning forward, Wyatt sticks his finger out and Zoey wipes it. She pricks his finger tip with the lancet, and he responds with an "Ouch!" Blood oozes out and she transfers two drops to the test card using the micro pipette, and follows up with a drop of buffer solution.

"We've to wait for twenty minutes."

Sweat forms on Wyatt's forehead as he sags in his chair, and Zoey repeats the process on herself.

They sit in silence and, after twenty minutes, she looks at the reading on Wyatt's test card.

"Negative!"

Wyatt releases a sigh of relief. "Phew!"

"Good for you!" Zoey stares with unblinking eyes at her own test card and within another minute, the reading appears.

"Negative, of course!"

"Great!" Wyatt looks at his watch. "I'm afraid your one hour's up." His lips bend in a wry smile. "Our time starts from the moment we met downstairs. If you want to play, you'll have to book another hour."

"In that case, not tonight." Zoey gingerly picks up the empty boxes and replaces their contents. "I'll call your agency's boss again in about a month's time."

Staring at the computer screen, Zoey reads the pages of a medical website about fertility. *Tracking your ovulation. Work out the length of your average menstrual cycle. Day one is the first day of the menstrual period and the last day is the day before the next period begins …*

She scrolls down. *Good …An ovulation calculator!* She inputs the information and clicks "Submit". A message appears in the answer box: "Your next most fertile period is Sunday February 11 to Tues February 13th." She reaches for her handphone and calls Wyatt's agency. "Hello? I want to book Wyatt again, next Sunday, 8 pm."

Four months later …

Wyatt goes to the men's toilet in the shopping mall where Hawaii Fitness is located and enters a cubicle. "Hello, Zoey? It's me, Wyatt." He unbuttons his pants and pulls his briefs to his knees with one hand. "I haven't heard from you after our third appointment, so I was wondering if you've forgotten about me. Err, I mean, are you happy with my service?" He lowers the toilet seat and sits down on it.

"Yes, I've no complaints about your service. But I won't need it any longer. I've got the result I wanted."

"How do you mean?" Wyatt rests his elbows on his knees.

"I'm pregnant." A chortle rolls from her lips.

"What!" Wyatt's arse-hole contracts in shock. "I … I'm very confused. You planned to get pregnant by me, didn't you?"

"Yes, you're right."

"But why? Remember, I said no child maintenance." He strains his rectal muscles and a piece of poop slides out.

"Don't worry, I don't want your money. Just to satisfy your curiosity, I'll explain the situation I was trapped in to you …"

Seven months earlier …

"David, please meet Zoey," Andrew says. "She's my fiancee." He casts a sideways glance at Zoey.

David smiles and offers his hand, which she clasps firmly for a moment. "Glad you could come to my son's birthday party."

"Since I'm going to be part of the family, I might as well get to know everyone."

"So, when's the wedding?" David's gaze darts from Zoey to Andrew.

"We'll set a date once Zoey and I find a suitable condo." Andrew slings an arm over his fiancee's shoulder. "Last week, we viewed a unit in Andaman Quayside. It's sea-facing with excellent sunset views. The agent quoted me one point three million, but we're still considering others."

"Ah, the birthday boy is here!" David looks up the staircase and Zoey follows his gaze.

A boy of about ten or eleven is taking slow steps down the carpeted staircase.

His eyes are slanted upward, his neck is thicker than normal and his tongue is almost bulging out of his mouth. He strolls towards his father.

David squats down and swallows his son in a hug. "New clothes? You look handsome!"

"P-Papa," the boy stutters, saliva drooling out of his mouth. "Y-You bought me w-what I asked for?"

"Yes, of course, son."

Zoey looks at the boy with pitiful eyes. *Poor thing! He's born with Down syndrome.*

Andrew looks out the front glass door. "My youngest brother's here with his family." The outside gate swings open and a family of four walks in.

A man is carrying a little girl whose head is slumped over his shoulder. One of his arms is wrapped around the girl's waist and the other is supporting her buttocks. The girl's legs are jerking uncontrollably. They enter the hall, followed by a woman and a boy, about six or seven years old.

"Oh my goodness!" Andrew moves towards the man. "Another epileptic seizure?"

He strokes the little girl at the back of the head.

"Yes, in the car!" The woman shoos away three kids sitting on the soft. "Go sit elsewhere, boys. Daisy has to lie down."

Zoey's face blanches and she purses her lips. *My goodness! Youngest brother's daughter also has some genetic condition.* The pity for the Down syndrome-boy in Zoey's heart turns to concern. *I think something genetically off runs in the family. My future child may be born with Down syndrome or some other unfortunate syndrome. I can't take the risk! What can I do? There must be a way out.*

"Is Zoey from Penang?" I ask, grabbing strands of Mamak mee goreng with my chopsticks.

"Possibly from the island." Wyatt sips at his 7-Up. "That's why she chose a hotel on the mainland. If she's out-of-state, very likely she'd have stayed in George Town." He looks at my plate. "How's the mee goreng?"

"Excellent." I chew and take a swallow. "Do you regret having fathered an illegitimate child?"

"No, no regrets at all. I know that she or he will have a good life."

"I wonder how will Zoey's husband will react when the child doesn't resemble him?"

"Oh, she had everything planned out. She picked me after going through several sources of male escorts. She said I resemble her husband slightly – lanky, long face, thin lips and fair-skinned."

* * *

Krishnan (not his real name), a graphic designer of an advertising agency, picks up the envelope left on his office desk by the peon earlier when he was out for lunch. It is marked "Private & Confidential". He tears open the envelope, pulls out a letter from his bank and starts to read it. *Please be informed that your minimum payment is overdue ...Arrrgh, shit!* He crumples the letter and tosses it into the waste-paper basket under his desk. *Where am I going to find more money?* He releases a sigh of frustration.

At home, Krishnan sits at his computer and types "vacancies for male escorts, Penang, Malaysia" in his favourite search engine. He clicks on the first result on his list. A window opens and an online classified ad states: "Join our male escort agency. We have ready male clients and sugar daddies all over Malaysia." *Yucks! I'm not gay!* He closes the window.

He refines his search and types "male escort seeking sugar mummies, Penang, Malaysia."A click on the mouse brings him to an advertisement by Bold & Handsome, a male-escort agency. He reads it mentally: *Earn as much as RM4,000 per week! High-society ladies in major towns seeking toy boys and sugar boys!*

Find your sugar mummy! Full discretion guaranteed! Call this number now! He reaches for his handphone and taps its screen. *I hope this part-time work will solve my financial woes.*

"Hello? Bold & Handsome, Christopher speaking."

Sounds like a Chinese. "I'm calling regarding your online ad, you know, this sugar mummy thing."

"You want to join us?"

"Yes, but I need more information."

"How old are you?"

"Twenty six, I'm Indian. You accept Indians?"

"Of course! We've many wealthy Indian women who are bored housewives and over-sexed Indian widows looking for a good time. Where're you calling from?"

"George Town, Penang."

"Can we meet up to discuss this? I'd like to assess you in person."

"Sure, how about this Saturday? 10 a.m?"

"Okay, we'll meet in Gurney Plaza, Kookaburra Café, ground floor. May I know your name?"

"Krishnan."

"I'll see you then. Bye."

"In the escort business, you must satisfy your client emotionally as well as physically," Christopher says, sitting upright across from Krishnan. "That means giving them a high BFE – that's short for boyfriend experience." He takes his hand off the iPad resting on his lap and lifts up his cup of cappuccino. "You understand?" He takes a small sip and puts the cup down.

Krishnan scratches his head. "Do you have a website?"

"In fact, we do but only members can access it." Christopher puts his iPad on the table. "Let me show you." He touches the screen a few times. "See? These are our male escorts." He slides the iPad towards Krishan. "There ...you see? We've men of all races, and they're earning good money." He leans back in his seat. "In our database, we've more than three hundred female clients." He gesticulates with his hands. "What we do is ...when a new escort joins us, we do an email blast to our members including shooting text messages to their handphones."

"Can I reject a booking? I mean if the woman's too old or too ugly."

"Wait, let me finish first." Christopher raises an open palm. "We're also connected with tour agencies. When foreign women travelling alone are here, the tour agencies will market our services to them – discreetly, of course." He raises two fingers. "We only take twenty percent of your fees. To join us, a registration fee of five hundred ringgit is required – this is a one-time payment. You also have to supply us two photographs: face and full-length." He leans forward and rests his hands on the table. "Now to answer your previous question, yes, you can reject a booking, but it's not advisable because end of the day, word gets round, and among our clients, you'll get a bad reputation."

"I see."

"So, can I welcome you to our agency?"

"I haven't got the money now."

"Don't worry." Christopher fishes out a ball pen and a used shopping receipt from his shirt pocket. "I'll give you our bank account number, and you can make a deposit at your convenience." He scribbles the bank account on the paper and hands it over to Krishnan.

Two days later, Krishnan dials Christopher's number. "Hello, Christopher? I'm Krishnan, I just deposited the payment in your account. Tonight, I'll email you my photos."

"Thank you and welcome aboard. In a few days' time when your photos are up on our website, I'll give you the access code, so you can have a look. Bye."

A week passes. Not having received any news from Christopher, Krishnan calls him. *Odd, there's no answer.* He tries repeatedly. Always, there is one ring tone and his call is diverted to voicemail. Alas, cruel reality slaps him on the face. *How stupid can I get! My number has been blocked! I've been scammed! Chuni warker!"*

* * *

Mustapha (not his real name) steers his car to the gate of a bungalow in Bukit Jambul, Penang. He picks up his mobile hand from the passenger seat and dials a number. "Faridah sweetheart, I'm home." The porch lights come on and the wrought-iron gate swings inward. Mustapha drives inside the front porch and gets out of the car.

A broad woman is standing in the front doorway. Her forehead is only three inches between her flat nose and her hair twisted into a pile of topknot. She is dressed in a long sleeved scoop-neck dress, and her face is bare of makeup.

Mustapha walks to the threshold of the front door and slips off his shoes.

Faridah steps aside. "How was work today, darling?" Her voice sounds like the caw of a crow.

"Great!" Mustapha enters the living room and stands close to her. "My boss complimented me on my presentation."

"Your favourite dishes are ready." Faridah turns her head sideways, waiting to be kissed. "I cooked them, not the maid."

Mustapha bends to press his lips against her chubby cheek, and she pulls back to reward him with a broad smile. Then, she steps away from him to close the grille door. When she has done so, Mustapha takes her pudgy hand and leads her across the hall to the dining area where a wash basin is located. They wash their hands and move to the dining area. Faridah lifts up the food cover and says, "The way to a man's heart is through his stomach!" She scoops rice onto two plates.

"Truer words have never been spoken." Mustapha seats himself, transfers a sambal prawn from a platter to his plate and starts to de-shell it. "Come, darling, let me feed you." He brings the prawn to her mouth.

Reny, the Indonesian maid, presses her ear against one wall of her bedroom. *Fuyoh! The bed's rattling like there's an earthquake inside!* The corners of her lips upturn in a grin. *I hope Puan Faridah doesn't squirt this time ....the bed sheet was a mess last time she had sex.* Reny continues to listen. Minutes pass. *She's groaning already, going to come very soon.* Reny clamps her lips tight to stave off a chuckle. *I better get back to the kitchen to do the dishes.* Reny steals to the door, eases it open and slips out of the room. She patters on her soles of her feet down the staircase to the kitchen.

Faridah stands outside the en-suite bathroom and lifts her arms slightly at her sides. Mustapha starts to dry her with a white cotton towel. He works on her papaya-shaped saggy breasts and moves down to her cellulite-packed hips and her massive thighs. Finally, he wipes her feet.

"You've cute feet, dear." Mustapha tosses the towel on the bed, picks up another towel and starts to dry himself. "Did I make you happy, darling?"

Faridah lumbers to a clothes hanger to pick up her scoop-neck dress. "Yes, you've satisfied me tremendously." She steps into the dress, takes Mustapha's clothes off the hanger and tosses them on the bed.

While Mustapha is putting on his clothes, Faridah goes to the dresser, tugs out a drawer and takes out some money notes. "You've played your role well." She moves toward Mustapha, now fully dressed and sitting on the bed. "I still miss my late husband, but you're a good surrogate." She hands him the money and turns her back to face him. Mustapha rises to his feet and pulls up the zipper at the back. They leave the bedroom with clinging hands.

An hour later, Mustapha enters his flat in Jelutong. As he swings the front door inward, he sees his wife, Zaiton, watching TV in the living room. A knot tangles in his stomach.

Her eyes light up and she jerks upright. Mustapha moves to where she's sitting, takes out some fifty-ringgit notes and gives them to her. "Here's the extra allowance you asked for." His tone is dry.

"Ah! Thank you! Now I can buy a new dress already!" Zaiton puts the money in her pajama shirt pocket. "Night auditor work at Marigold Hotel again?"

"No." Mustapha starts to stride to the master bedroom. "Tonight was at Kemboja Inn – their staff's on leave."

"You must work harder, darling."

You should spend less! Not bothering to answer her, Mustapha eases the door open and enters the bedroom, closing the door silently behind him, his cool manner masking the seething inside.

Mustapha gives a sad shake of his head. "I don't enjoy being a male escort!" He flicks his gaze to a stunner passing our table and back to me. "When Zaiton and I were dating, she was thrifty. Now she has changed, possibly due to influence from friends."

I stir my glass of grass jelly with soya bean. "Haven't you tried other part-time work?"

"I was a part-time despatch rider, but the pay was chicken feed. Escorting earns fast and easy money."

"What will happen if your wife finds out about your escorting work?"

"I think she'll divorce me." He takes a sip of his Soda Gembira. "But if I don't give her the extra money she asks for, she'll also divorce me, eventually." His lips blow out a gust of frustration. "I guess I married the wrong woman."

6

Mamasans of Patpong

As tuk-tuks, taxis, cars and motorbikes pass by me, they belch grey exhaust fumes, which almost choke me. Traipsing along the pavement of Sukhumvit Soi 22, I come to Canary Bar (not its real name) in a side alley. The accordion metal shutter door is opened partway to reveal an aluminum-framed split glass door at the right of the bar's frontage. A CLOSED sign is hanging on the inside. I cup one hand and peer in through the glass. The back portion of the hall is lighted to reveal a bar counter and I step sideways to ring the doorbell. Before I can jab the button, a voice behind me says: "The bar is closed. Are you looking for someone?" Her English is accented.

I turn to see a Thai sweet thing, probably mid-twenties, garbed in a short-sleeved T-shirt and denim jeans standing on the fringe of my private space. Her right hand is carrying a big tote bag.

"I've appointment with Mummy Sukhon."

The lass jabs a few buttons on a key pad on a wall and the door clicks open. "You can come in."

We step inside a dimly lit hall. She disappears through a doorway at the back and moments later, Mummy Sukhon shows up, striding on low heels. Her curvy figure is togged up in a beige midi dress with Thai tattoo designs, which makes her cinnamon complexion look lighter. She is probably in her early thirties, and her shoulder-length hair has a part in the middle.

"Ah, Jackson, you're on time." Her thin lips tilt in a welcome smile. "I'm sorry I didn't hear the doorbell. I was in the ladies. In fact, I arrived five minutes ago." She gestures with an open palm to a low-backed bar stool. "Please take a seat. I've to do something – my routine ritual."

Last night, three attempts to secure interviews in Soi Cowboy failed because the mamasans were too busy attending to business instead of to a trivial matter like telling their life stories for "an academic research paper," as I had put it. So, I moseyed to lower Sukhumvit, a quieter area, and ended in Canary Bar. I had a couple of drinks here, chatted with Sukhon, who's the owner-cum-mamasan, and requested for an interview. She agreed and asked me to come the next day at 6 p.m., which is an hour before the bar's opening time.

Now, Mummy Sukhon goes behind the bar, takes out a pint glass and sets it on the counter with a thud. She grabs a whisky bottle by the neck and starts to fill up one-third of the pint glass. The Thai girl who spoke to me earlier takes long strides to a side wall and taps on a switch. A metal wall light behind the bar illuminates to reveal a small wooden altar shaped like a half-cylinder resting on a shelf. With two flicks of her forefinger, Mummy opens the two doors of the altar. My eyes bulge in shock. A wooden phallus, which is six inches high and about two inches in diametre is standing vertically inside the altar. The next instant, my cheeks feel hot from embarrassment.

Stepping towards the altar, Mummy Sukhon picks up a joss stick from a bunch and lights it. She bows to the wooden phallus with both hands holding the joss-stick and plants it in a small copper urn. Footfalls make me flit my gaze to the doorway at the end of the hall. Five girls troop out and hover near the front of the hall, as if waiting for a cue from their mamasan.

Mummy Sukhon picks up the wooden phallus and dips it repeatedly in the pint glass held in her other hand. Now, she strides towards the front doorway, which has been opened by the girl who spoke to me earlier. Mummy taps the perimeter of the door frame repeatedly with the wooden phallus. The sight almost makes my jaw drop. Then she stands in the doorway with her back facing outside. After a quick left and right gaze to make sure the coast is clear, she tosses the whisky over her shoulder, which splashes onto the pavement.

Mummy Sukhon goes to the cash register at one end of the bar counter and taps it with the wooden phallus several times. She jabs a button and the cash drawer shoots out with a ding. She takes out a few money notes and slaps them to her forehead. After returning the money notes to the cash register, she returns to her former position in the doorway with the wooden phallus. Facing outside, she bends over and spreads her legs wide. Her stable of six bargirls line up behind her, each girl holding the waist of the one in front. Mummy holds the wooden phallus, taps it on the floor three times and sends it sliding on the floor between her legs, including those of the girls. The ritual object clatters against the wall at the far end of the hall.

Mummy retrieves the wooden phallus, bustles about to tap

the round wooden tables and high stools. Then she returns to her position at the front of the line, passes the wooden phallus around her left thigh and uses it to outline the male genitalia on the floor before passing it under her legs to the next girl. The second girl repeats what Mummy has done and eventually the ritual object ends at the end of the line where Mummy has now stationed herself. She takes the object and replaces it on the altar. Her stable of girls disperse. End of ritual.

"Come, let's go to my office." Mummy Sukhon traipses past the doorway at the end of the hall with me and a few girls in tow, their heels clicking on the floor.

We walk down a short corridor between partitioned rooms and Mummy stops at a door with an upper glass panel, while the other girls squeeze past us to proceed ahead and enter another room on the left.

Mummy Sukhon and I enter her office and I plunk my butt on the visitor's chair while she rounds her desk to her swivel chair. She picks up a remote control on her desk, points it at the air-con at one wall and clicks. Beep! She sits up ramrod straight. "Can I get you a drink?" Her pointed chin makes her face resembles a crescent moon.

"I just took my dinner at Khing Klao, just down the road."

"So, Jackson, what do you want to know?" Her big brown eyes assess me with curiosity. "Last night, you told me you're doing a research paper."

I cross my legs at the ankles. "Before I answer your question, what was that ritual all about?"

"It's to bring good luck and customers to my bar."

"All bars do it?"

"No, if you believe in it, you do it."

"I see." I lean forward in my chair. "Back to your question – can you tell me what brought you to Patpong?"

"Oh? I see." Mummy Sukhon leans back on the headrest of her swivel chair and so begins her story ...

More than a decade earlier ...

Phonphan and her 18-year-old daughter Sukhon step into the porch of their wooden house and take off their pointed straw hats. For four hours, they were bent double in the paddy field, harvesting the golden stalks. The one-hectare paddy field they are working on is sprawled in the outskirt of Korat, Nakhon Ratchatsima Province, and Phonphan's husband is a share cropper.

As she fans herself with her hat, Sukhon strides past his father's battered motorcycle propped up on its stand. "Eh, *Phx* has come back." She unlocks the front wooden door, kicks off her sandals and enters the living room.

Phonphan turns the doorknob to her bedroom and pushes the door open. She sees her husband lying on the scruffy mattress of their bed. "Dusit , what's wrong with you?" She strides to the bed. "Didn't you go to work on the plantation?" The wooden bed creaks as she sits on its edge.

To supplement his income, her husband recently secured contract work to harvest sugar cane in a plantation. The sugar cane stalks are then supplied to a refinery in Korat.

A gravelly groan drags from Dusit's lips. "I – I came back early." He grimaces and presses an open palm his chest. "I've pain in my chest."

"You need to see a doctor."

"B -but I've no ...money."

"What?" Phonpan's eyes span wider in shock. "Weren't you paid wages a fortnight ago?" She releases a heavy exhale. "You've been gambling again? And lost?" She gives a slow shake of her head. "Your health's not good because you smoke and drink too much."

His face contorted in pain, Dusit does not answer but continues to inhale and exhale in staggers.

Phonphan goes to the dining room to find Sukhon sitting at the rattan table eating rice with vegetable curry and salted fish. She joins her daughter and scoops some rice from a battered aluminum container. As she chews on her food, her gaze travels to Sukhon's full lips and down to her big breasts straining the cotton shirtdress.

For a few moments, Phonphan's eyes take on a faraway quality and then she swallows her food. "Sukhon, after your lunch, go take a bath." Her gaze meets Sukhon's for a few moments. "Change into a nice dress. We're going to cycle to Korat, find some money."

Two hours later, Phonphan and Sukhon step into a beer bar at Suepsiri Road in Korat. Several Thai customers are sitting at a table, taking advantage of the cheaper prices during Happy Hours. A dozen curious eyes glare at them but the attention is focused on Sukhon whose tight dress reveals the curves of her young figure.

Earlier, Phonphan and Sukhon visited two other bars along the same road. In the first bar, there was only a local drunk slumped face-down on a table. The second bar had two *farang* customers but Phonphan could not speak English and she asked the barman to act as interpreter. When he heard when Phonphan said, he gave her a tongue-lashing and ordered her to leave.

Presently, Phonphan approaches the nearest table where a stocky man with a shiny pate is sitting with his scrawny friend. "Mister," she half-whispers to the stocky man. "I want to sell my daughter to you – short time." The tone of her voice contains hidden guilt tempered with desperation.

The stocky man's lecherous gaze roves from Sukhon's shapely thighs below the hemline to her shin and to her feet, shod in sandals. "Are you sure?" He licks his rubbery lips and slashes his hand through his thinning hair in excitement.

Phonphan casts a furtive glance at the barman who's washing mugs at a sink at one end of the bar and nods.

"How old is she?"

"Eighteen."

"Show me proof that she's eighteen."

Phonphan turns to her daughter. "Sukhon, give me your I.D. card." She extends her hand.

With quivering hands, Sukhon takes out her I.D. card, hands it to her mother, and it ends up in the fatso's hands.

"I want a piece of the action, too," the scrawny man hisses. Fidgeting in his seat, he leans forward and cranes his neck to look at Sukhon's I.D. card in his friend's hand. "Can you let me be first?"

The stocky man shoots a serious gaze to his friend with a spike of brows. "No, I want to be first!" A scornful grin curls his lips. "You can be second! After all, her mother approached me, not you."

The three people negotiate and come to an agreed price and a nearby short-time hotel. "Payment first," Phonphan says, her eyes glinting with impatience, "when we reach the hotel lobby."

The two men glug down their beers and get down from their bar stools. "Come, my car's parked outside," says the stocky man, dipping a hand into his trouser pocket to fish out his car keys.

Phonphan turns to Sukhon. "My dear, we're going with these kind gentlemen. You have to be obedient to them, okay?" She steers Sukhon by the waist to the doorway. "There's no need to be afraid. I'll go with you to the hotel and wait downstairs."

A tremor of nervousness rattles Sukhon's body. "Y-yes, *Mae*." Her voice is on the edge of cracking.

When Phonphan and Sukhon return home, the sky is bleeding colours on the horizon just as the latter is bleeding between her thighs. Overhead, the sky is specked with the silhouettes of birds flying home. Phonphan's son has returned from school as indicated by his bicycle parked in the front porch.

Skittish with excitement, Phonphan takes long strides past the living room and overhears her son reading aloud from his room. She steps into her bedroom and announces, "Dusit! Dusit! We've money – when you want to go to the hospital?" Her husband is lying on his side with his back facing her and she settles down on the edge of the bed. "Dusit?" There is no reply.

"Dusit?" Gripping her husband's shoulder, she turns him face up. She recoils as shards of shock slashes her gut. Her husband's fish-like eyes stare at the ceiling, and he remains motionless.

"Oh Lord Buddha! He's dead!" Tears stream down Phonphan's face.

A year passes ...

Her hair pulled back in a ponytail with little-girl bangs, Sukhon sticks her head in a gap in the doorway of Somchai Go-Go Bar in a side alley in Patpong and sees a matronly woman mopping the floor. "Excuse me, I saw your vacancies sign outside and – ."

"Come in." The woman steps to the doorway and pulls the scissor grille door wider for Sukhon to enter. "Go to the back and talk to Mr. Somchai, first room." She returns to her former spot and continues to mop.

Scrunching her nose at the sting of stale cigarette smoke, Sukhon weaves past tables and enters a doorway at the back of the hall. In the first cubicle, she sees Somchai, probably in his forties, through the glass door. He is hunched forward over his desk, with a file in front of him, and jabbing buttons on a calculator. Sporting penitentiary haircut, he has on a short-sleeved shirt with a top button undone.

Upon hearing a knock on the door, he looks up and flaps an open palm. "Yes? Come in."

Sukhon steps in the room, bows at the man with her palms pressed together. "I understand you've vacancies for bargirls."

Somchai gestures to an empty chair across him. "Your name?"

Sukhon drags the chair out, sits and rests her hands on her

lap. "My name's Sukhon Sompong."

Somchai pushes his calculator and file to one side. "So, you want to work here?" Leaning forward, he splays his hands on the table.

"Yes."

"Where're you from?"

"Korat."

"Any experience?"

Sukhon shakes her head, her ponytail quivering with the motion. "No."

"Why you want to work here?"

"I hope to meet a nice man so I can marry him."

Somchai's lips suddenly crack in a grin to reveal nicotine-stained teeth. "Money! You come here to earn big money! That's the truth, right?" His grin blooms into a smile. "Why do eight out of ten girls who come here say that crap about finding a husband?"

Blood rushes to Sukhon's cheeks and her face feels hot.

Somchai's smile subsides along with the jest in the tone of his voice. "Anyway, let's get down to business." The tone of his voice becomes serious. "Our vacancies for bargirls and go-go dancers are still not filled." He pauses to take an inhale. "Let me explain the differences. A go-go dancer is paid a higher basic than a bargirl. Then again, there are two types of go-go dancers. Naked and fully clothed. By naked, I mean wearing G-string but topless." He points to the ceiling. "Naked dancers dance upstairs on the first floor. As for bargirls, unofficially, I divide them into two types: the beautiful and average-looking. The beauties are stationed at the outside tables at the pavement, and the ugly, err, I mean, unlovely girls are inside. This is a marketing gimmick to lure in customers. All bars practise this tactic. To be honest, it can get quite hot outside." He gives a slow nod of his head. "Both bargirl and go-go dancer get the same commission on lady's drink and barfine." He raises his right forefinger. "A girl will be put on one month's probation. Upon confirmation in the second month, she has to hit quotas on lady's drink and barfine. First month, no quotas."

"What happens if quotas are not met?"

"Her salary will be deducted, based on a sliding scale." He hikes his stubby chin. "You're still interested?"

Sukhon squints her eyes in thought for a moment. "Yes, but can I try as a bargirl first? Later, I may hop to being a naked go-go dancer."

Reporting for work on her first day, Sukhon is taken to Mummy Karawek's tiny cubicle.

"You speak English?" Mummy Karawek asks, shooting her an enquiring gaze across a scuffed wooden desk.

Seated upright, Sukhon forms a two-inch gap between her thumb and forefinger. "A little bit."

Mummy Karawek's lips slant downward in a scowl. "That won't do, we've many *farang* customers in our bar." She pulls out a side drawer, which screeches and takes out an A5-size booklet and three cardboard boxes of different sizes. "You need this book to improve your English." She spreads out the boxes and book in front of her. "I'll let you have a copy of the book. It contains useful phrases and words that're related to your work." She turns the book top side up to Sukhon.

Sukhon looks at the front cover and reads the title, "Get-Rich-Quick English for Bar Girls".

Mummy Karawek nods. "Now, pulling in a customer is easy but making him stay inside for as long as possible requires a little effort. One way is to keep him entertained, you understand?" She raises her eyebrows. "To start off, you can invite him to pay common bar games with you." She taps a rectangular box about the size of a dictionary. "This is Jengka, a simple game of building blocks." She opens the second box to reveal a plastic frame with holes and a rubble of red and yellow discs. "Now, this is Connect Four and – " her hand gestures to the third unopened box – "this is Flippet. I'll explain how to play these games now; tomorrow I'll go through the book with you. You'll shine in your job if you memorize those phrases."

"So that was my first day at work." Mummy Sukhon rises from her chair, goes to a filing cabinet and takes out a booklet about A5 in size. She steps forward to hand it to me and sinks back in her chair, whose springs squeal.

I look down at the booklet in my hands. It's a copy of *Get-Rich-Quick English for Bar Girls*. The front cover is slightly worn, its top right corner dog-eared. "Great balls of fire! You kept the book after more than a decade?"

"Yes, this book changed my life."

I lean back in my chair, flick through a few of the contents pages, and read them mentally. *Private Time page 59-80. Our*

Body page 81-83. Sexual Vocabulary page 85-88. At the Restaurant and Bar page 89-94. Excuses for Not Going with Men page 95-96. I turn to the chapter titled "Sexual Vocabulary". The words *bite, groan, hug, insert, kiss, lick* alongside Thai text leap up to my eyes. I clamp my lips tight to stave off a grin, snap the book shut and return it to Mummy. "Very useful indeed. Any unforgettable men you met in your first bar? Or any other bars."

"Two years later, I met a *farang* who became my husband when I was working in another bar in Silom Road." Mummy Sukhon's voice is as tender as the look in her eyes.

From the doorway of a bar on Silom Road, Frank (not his real name) hears the sexy strains of a saxophone and stop to look at a promotional poster on a metal standee outside: JIM JAZZ CLUB: 20% DISCOUNT ON BEERS. The road ahead is chock-a-block with nightspots emblazoned with countless neon signs, and the setting sun is dyeing the sky pomegranate pink.

Frank turns to walk away and bumps into a Thai doll carrying a paper cup in one hand and a tote bag in the other. Their bodies collide, crushing the paper cup and spilling the contents. The Thai girl takes a step backward as coffee spills on her pink dress that ends at her knees.

"Oh, why don't you watch where you're going?" Her silky voice is calm.

"Oh, I'm so sorry." Frank gives her an apologetic grimace. "Err, how much will it cost to clean the dress at the launderette? I'll pay for the cleaning cost."

"I don't know, but I have to report for work inside." She

gives her long hair a toss. "I'm already late."

Frank hikes his chin in the direction of the doorway. "You work in the bar?"

"Yes, I'm a hostess." The girl's big eyes framed by curly lashes contain a sensuous flame. "Why don't you come in? After I've changed to my work clothes, I can pass you my stained dress. You can take it to the nearest launderette down the road. It's near I-Sleep Silom Hostel. Ask for express service and they'll clean it for you within an hour. You can come back and return the dress to me."

Frank's tight expression relaxes into a smile. "I'll be happy to buy you another cup of coffee as well."

"Oh, please do, I need it to stay awake. It's Thai civet coffee." She extends a hand with varnished finger nails. "I'm Sukhon." Her slender fingers clasp Frank's outstretched hand warmly. "How shall I address you?"

"Frank, Frank Harris."

They enter a hall where jazz saxophone tunes are seeping from speakers, which burrow into every nook and cranny. At one end of the hall stands a small stage, and the rest of the space is taken up by chairs and round tables.

Sukhon gestures to the nearest chair. "Please take a seat." She claps a hand on Frank's shoulder as he sits down. "I won't be long."

A waiter holding a menu starts to walk up to Frank but goes away after Sukhon speaks something to him in Thai language. She then disappears through a door at the back and reappears five minutes later. As she saunters towards Frank with a small paper bag in her hand, his jaw sags. The transformation from girl-next-door to sex kitten stuns him: stilettos, deep cleavage, satiny brown thighs and a pair of kissable of crimson lips.

"Oh blimey!" Frank mutters to himself. "She has more curves than a mountain road!" His gaze swept over Sukhon from head to toe, and his nose savours the fragrance of ylang ylang from her perfume.

"Here you are." The edge of Sukhon's mouth crooks into a smile as she hands over the bag to Frank. "I'll be working till 3 a.m. Try to be back as soon as you can just in case someone bar-fines me out."

An hour later, Frank returns to Sukhon's club and hands her a plastic bag containing her dress, still smelling of fabric softener.

Sukhon takes the plastic bag and places a gentle palm on Ian's cheek. "Oh thank you, darling, you're such a sweet gentleman." Smiling, she gives a playful pinch on his cheek. "I'll go keep this in my locker but I'll be back. So, why don't you take a table?"

Ten minutes later, Sukhon and Frank are engaged in a tete-a-tete in a dark corner of the club. She loops an arm over his neck and moves closer to him on the settee. "Frank, please tell me something about yourself."

"Oh shucks, there's nothing much to tell. I'm a dairy farmer in Somerset, England ..."

The room-service waiter jabs the doorbell with one hand, his other carrying a tray laid with two plates of pineapple fried rice.

The door swings inward and the waiter steps in. At that moment, a *farang* shuffles out of the bathroom, with a pair of black lacy bra tied around his eyes. Wearing only boxers, he stretches out his arms and calls, "Yuhoooo ...where are you Sukhon?"

Oh my goodness! A farang playing blind man's bluff with a bargirl! Stifling a chortle, the waiter displays a stony face with much effort.

From behind the door, a Thai girl steps forward. "Please leave the tray on the writing desk." Her chiffon see-through lingerie triggers a blast of heat from his groin.

"Frank was twenty-five years older than me." Sukhon's eyelashes flip up with the faintest of smile. "But he was young at heart."

"Was?"

"A year later, he sold his Somerset farm, moved to Bangkok and married me." She tugs stray strands of hair behind her ear. "He bought a townhouse in Min Buri and started this beer bar with me as his partner. Business was okay. One day, three years after our marriage, he rode his motorcycle out to run some errands and, a few hours later, the police came. They said that Frank had been involved in a terrible accident with a lorry." Her throat convulses with a choking swallow. "I ... I was pregnant with our first child." She looks down at the floor, unwilling to let me see her eyes. "A week after his funeral, I suffered a miscarriage." Seconds pass before she looks up, and when she does, her eyes are red-rimmed.

"I'm sorry, I brought back sad memories." I take out a small plastic packet of tissue from my pocket. "I think it's time for me to leave." I tug one piece out and hand it over to Sukhon.

"Thanks." Her voice is waterlogged.

* * *

Mummy Boonsri and three handsome hunks with charming smiles plastered on their faces stand facing Namthip (not her real name), who's sitting on a plush settee. "Good evening, Miss, it's good to see you again." Stepping forward gingerly in her heels, Mummy plops beside Namthip, causing the cushions to whoosh. "These are our new hosts, you've seen the rest of them before." Mummy pauses for a reaction but there is none so she knows her client isn't interested to view the other men. "Now, from left to right." She gestures to a handsome European man togged up in a snazzy suit. "This is Pierre from France, speaks good English, twenty-eight years old, six-month modeling contract in Bangkok, a part-timer here." Her gaze flits to the next man who clasps his palms together and performs a *wai*. "Next host is a Thai, university student, part-timer, dances well, loves to karaoke. His name's Naowarat." Taking an inhale, Mummy pauses and shifts slightly in her seat. "And, we've a rare black diamond from Africa – Obasi!" At the mention of his name, the African flashes a smile, revealing teeth whiter than rice-white. "From Nigeria; he's only twenty years old – very strong and accommodating. All three men give excellent BFE!"

Namthip, aged 33, is in Bovary Club (not its real name), a male-host club in Ratchadapisek district. She is dressed in a sleeveless floral print dress, which accentuates every roll of fat in her body. Still single, she runs her own interior decorating firm and smokes, drinks and loves parties and fast cars. Big eyes the colour of shellack assess the men standing in front of her while a tingle travelling down from her navel to her crotch begins to intensify into a quiver. "Hmm ...I think I'll take Pierre." Her chubby cheeks reveal dimples as she speaks. "And, tonight, I want my regular wine, a plate of spring rolls and one box of Marlboro Lights." She turns to Pierre who has now plopped down on the settee beside her, his arm looped around her waist. "Darling, what do you want to eat and drink?"

Three hours later, at the nightclub's closing time, Mummy Boonsri appears and deposits a silver platter with a bill in front of Namthip, her face flushed with the warmth of alcohol, her crotch burning with the flames of desire.

Namthip takes out her purse from her handbag and pulls out a credit card. "Please keep my unfinished wine for my next visit." She tosses the card on the silver platter, her pulse quickening at the thought of Pierre in her arms soon in her usual love motel.

"Will do." Mummy lowers herself on her knees to grab the wine bottle by the neck with one hand and scrunches her nose momentarily in thought. "Miss Namthip, since you're our regular customer, why don't you open an account here?" She picks up the silver platter with her other hand. "You can settle your amount outstanding at the end of every month, and we don't charge interest, so it's cheaper than using credit card." Her eyes hold a warm invitation. "You can come to my office anytime tomorrow. I'll let you fill in some forms. On your next visit, you can just sign the bill."

Eight months later ...

"Mr. Apichet, please understand my situation," Namphit pleads, her eyes entreating his. "My business is not doing well. I haven't secured any big projects for the past four months, the economy's not good." Her voice is choked with emotion. "And please don't send your thugs to my office to harass me anymore."

Mr. Apichet, owner of Bovary Club, waves his gnarled right hand. "Spare me your problems!" He leans back in his swivel chair, ponders for a second and sits straight again. "Incidentally, I am co-owner of a social escort agency. I suggest you work for us as a social escort. You speak English well, and if you lose a few pounds, you'll be in demand by *farang* customers." He leans forward, places two clenched fists on his desk and shoots a piercing glare at Namphit. "In that way, you can clear off your debts quickly. What do you think?"

"Huh? Sleep with men twice my age? That's disgusting!" The air thins in her throat as reality strikes. "I like young men, not old grandfathers!"

"Do you have any choice?" Mr. Apichet's dark gaze contains a veiled sinister threat. "If it's any consolation, do the deed with the lights switched off. It feels the same whether with young man or old man."

Ending her story, Mummy Namthip drags on a cigarette, tilts her head upward and blows a few smoke rings. "So I enrolled in a slimming programme and lost about ten pounds." Her gaze fuses to mine for a moment as I take a glug of my beer and eye her over the rim of the mug. "At first, I did part-time escorting but later I closed down my interior decorating business to go full-time. After my debts were cleared, I started my own escort agency. Then I ventured into the bar business."

* * *

Sungei Golok, Thai-Malaysian border. December 2014

Looking out through the glass front façade from the inside, the mamasan of Summer KTV Bar (not its real name) sees a man getting out of a motorcycle taxi, which has stopped and he's stepping to the pavement. She rises from her stool behind the bar, scuttles towards the swing glass door to pull it inward.

A twenty-something-year-old man with the complexion of coffee lumbers in and the mamasan sizes him up. *Aha! A well-dressed customer, not a poor farmer.* "Good evening, sir!" A smile pulls at the corners of her mouth. "You're a lucky man tonight as we still have a karaoke room left." She casts a downward glance at his trouser legs, which are wet from the knees down. "My goodness, what happened?"

The man's lips edge into a sheepish half-smile. "When the boat stopped, I took a misstep and landed with two legs in the water!" His voice is guttural. "For obvious reasons, the boatman didn't want to shine any light."

"Come, choose your girlfriend first, wet pants will dry up, small problem." *Ah well, another illegal river crossing from Rantau Panjang in the middle of the night!* She steers him by a gentle nudge on his shoulder to a karaoke room, amongst a span of others, along one length of the hall. In the remaining open space, a few tables are occupied with drinkers and their hostesses.

Inside the karaoke room, the man plops down on a settee

and, within minutes, buxom Sasithorn is chosen amongst other tootsies as his hostess for the evening. "Oh darling, your trousers are wet!?" Sasithorn flits her gaze from his trouser legs to his eyes. "Why don't I dry them for you? There're several air-con compressors in the enclosed backyard. I can hang your trousers over a compressor and it'll dry them within minutes." She winks. "Don't be shy, more daring things have been done by men in karaoke rooms than removing their trousers."

"Being a veteran of hanky-panky karaoke, I'm not shy." The man rises to his feet, unbuckles his belt and steps out of his pants. "You deserve a fat tip after the night's over."

"Of course, I do." Sasithorn's eyes twinkle with a tease as she feigns a gawk at his crotch. "Ooooh … what a big bulge!" She takes the bundled-up trousers from him. "You want special service afterward?"

"Yes! I'll be waiting naked with open arms when you return. Let's do it when the night's still young."

To the chortle of her client, Sasithorn eases the door open a crack and slips out of the karaoke room. Clomping on wedges to the rear section of the bar, she drapes the trousers over an air-con compressor, which is discharging hot air and saunters back to the hall, yanking the back door open.

As she turns to close the door behind her after entering, a burst of yellow flames and a deafening boom rip through the hall. Her instinct makes her crouch on the floor, her heart battering her ribs. Bar stools and pieces of partitions from the karaoke rooms fly through the air amidst billowing smoke. A few women and men are screaming and rushing out of the bar through the back door. Several others are scampering out through the front door. As Sasithorn gets up on her feet, her client – his terrified face turned pale – bolts past her. He's stark naked and is only wearing his sandals!

Fast forward to the present ...

"See this scar?" Mummy Sasithorn lifts up her left arm and pulls down the sleeve with her right hand to reveal a keloid scar on her bicep. "A piece of broken glass cut me here, which needed several stitches." She pulls the sleeve back in place. "Luckily, I was at the far end of the hall, otherwise I might've been badly injured. A week after that bombing, I came to Bangkok, where it's safer." She chugs her beer with a tilt of her pilsner glass and licks her lips. "Golok is a dangerous town as insurgents are active there. They like to strike during Christmas and the Muslim fasting month." She knots the fingers of her hands together and places them on the bar counter. You've been to Golok?"

"No, but I'll be going to Hatyai soon."

Her delicate brows squish in apparent concern. "In Hatyai and Golok, don't go near motorcycles parked outside bars and discos. They may be fitted with bombs, which are detonated by handphones."

Mummy Sasithorn is sitting across me over a teak bar counter in a nightclub in Surawong Road during Happy Hours. She has on a half-sleeve tight dress, with her ample breasts overflowing the scoop neckline to create a deep valley. Her facial features are near-perfect: a well-rounded chin, a Cupid's bow on her upper lip and a pointed nose.

I toss my gaze from my pilsner glass to her big eyes. "How long have you been in Bangkok?"

"Four years already, and I'm happily married." She raises her pilsner glass. "*Chiyo!* [Cheers!].

"*Chiyo!*" I clink my pilsner glass to hers. "Married to a *farang*?" I take a token sip of my beer.

"No, a Thai businessman." She takes a swig and clunks her pilsner glass down. "This nightclub belongs to him and his partners; he also runs a spa. I'm his minor wife."

"Err, you mean second wife?"

"Yes." She nods with a nonchalant expression. "I met him when I was working as a hostess in a karaoke bar in Thonglor area. Those bars mostly cater to local Thais, unlike those in Patpong. He was a regular at my former place, and, after a short courtship, we got married. His first wife's barren and cannot bear him children so that's why he wanted a minor wife – to give him a child. At first, things didn't go smoothly as I suffered a miscarriage in the first year of our marriage. He was very upset. According to the doctor, my previous abortion when I was a teenager probably made it difficult for me to carry a baby to full term. Then I prayed at the Chao Mae Tubtim Temple and – success! – I bore him a son. He was so happy."

"What's this Chao Mae Temple?"

"It's also called Fertility Shrine. Hundreds of wooden penises are scattered in its compound. All different sizes, painted in various colours, and a few made of stone."

My eyebrows crimp in puzzlement. "Why so many phallic symbols there?"

"Women who want to conceive will first bring jasmine and lotus for the goddess. When their wishes come true, they will return to pray, and give a wooden penis as a token of gratitude." A glimmer of smile plays on her lips as she stretches her arms apart to the maximum. "Mine was five feet long and painted pink. My husband and his worker carried it to the temple for me."

I jerk upright in my seat. "Location of the temple?" I recall Mummy Sukhon's bar-opening ritual and ponder whether Thai women are afflicted with penis fetishes.

"Used to be in the compound of Swissotel Nai Lert Park."

"Sounds like a hotel? But I haven't heard of it."

"You've heard of David Carradine?"

"Yes, he was the star of the TV series *Kung Fu.*"

"David Carradine died in the Swissotel Nai Lert Park. Oh … that poor man, but his death made the hotel famous." The tone of her voice is laced with sympathy. "But the hotel has closed, and there're renovations to convert it into a hospital. So the temple has moved to the Nai Lert Heritage House."

"Is it nearby? The Heritage House, I mean."

"Yes, it's in Som Khit Alley, very near to the former Swissotel, about ten, fifteen minutes by taxi from here, depending on traffic."

"This temple I gotta see!" I lean forward in my bar stool. "Can you take me there?"

"When?"

"How about now?"

Mummy Sasithorn's voice turns dry. "It's only open to the public on Thursday and Friday."

"Bah! I'll be leaving Bangkok on Wednesday." I flick my wrist in front of me to read the time on my watch. "I've got to go." Shifting in the bar stool, I pull out my wallet from my trouser side pocket. "Thanks for talking with me, Mummy." I plunk payment on the counter for my bottle of Singha beer and climb down from the bar stool.

Mummy Sasithorn's lips upturn into a grin. "You're welcome." Quickly, she stretches out her arm and shows me her left open palm.

My jaw drops. On her palm are the words *My Tip?* which were written using a black marker pen.

7

Passage to Hell

Seventeen-year-old Sanit rushes to the kitchen of his wooden house in Khlong Toey, Bangkok's oldest slum. Ratree, his mother, looks up from the mortar filled with spices, which she's pounding.

"*Mae* [Mum], I got my examination results – I've secured second place in my class! I want to go to university and study economics!" He unloops the strap of his schoolbag from his shoulder and takes out a sheet of thick paper. "Here's my report card."

Her face covered with a sheen of sweat, Ratree takes the report card and reads it. "That's great, son." *Oh Lord Buddha! How am I going to find the money to pay for his university education?*

Three years ago, her husband was sentenced to fifteen years jail and fined 1.5 million baht for possession of 100 *yaba* pills [methamphetamine], which he intended to sell to Western tourists in the backpacker area of Khao San. He could not pay the fine and an additional two years was added to his sentence. Since his imprisonment, Ratree has been operating a street stall in Yaowarat, Bangkok's Chinatown.

A year later ...
Seated at his writing desk, Kraisee hears the front door of his room unlock. He looks up from the book he's reading. His room-

mate Sanit enters, closes the door behind him and slips off his sandals. "How's Professor Somkid's lecture today?" Kraisee asks.

Kraisee and Sanit are lodgers in the campus of Luangpaichit University (not its real name) in Bangkok.

Sanit goes to his bed, which is several feet away from Kraisee's and sits down. "Interesting as usual, peppered with jokes." He props his pillow against the headboard, leans back and pulls out an envelope folded in two from his shirt pocket.

Kraisee flips a page and looks down again. "Can we skip instant noodles this evening and eat outside?"

"Sure." Sanit tears open his envelope.

Kraisee turns on his chair to face Sanit. "Letter from girlfriend?"

"No, it's from my mother." Sanit pulls out two pieces of paper from the envelope and looks at them. "She has enclosed a bank draft for my next semester's fees." He unfolds a sheet of paper with Thai scripts. "There's also a letter from her." He starts to read the letter mentally.

"Where's she?"

Sanit casts his gaze at Kraisee for a tick. "In Pattaya."

"Doing what?"

"She's a cook in a twenty-four-hour fast-food restaurant." Sanit wriggles his toes. "An international burger chain."

"Huh? She can afford to send you here just by flipping burgers?"*She's probably a bargirl there. From the photo of her I saw in your wallet's plastic window, your mother's a hot MILF.*

"My mum works hard. She also runs a stall at Thepprasit Road Night Bazaar on weekends."

"Odd, I haven't heard you talk with her on your handphone before." *She seems* to *be a woman who works during the night, sleeps when the sun is up.*

"She's on the night-shift in the restaurant." He re-folds the letter. "I'll be visiting her during the semester break as I haven't been to Pattaya before."

"I see." Kraisee scratches the back of his head. "What about your house in Khlong Toei?" *That's just a wooden shack, two notches better than my dog's kennel.* "Who's staying there now?

"My mother rented it out."

Kraisee springs to his feet. "I need a break." He stretches out his arms. "Want to go for tea in the canteen now?"

Sanit replaces the letter and bank draft in the envelope. "Okay." He goes to his desk and keeps the envelope in its top drawer. "I hope their *khanom kip lamduan* are freshly baked today."

In Pattaya

Ratree mounts the last step of the staircase to the fourth-floor corridor and strides to her one-room apartment. Following her behind is Sanit, lugging a canvas knapsack on his back. Half an hour earlier, Ratree met her son at the main bus terminal in North Road and they took a taxi here: an apartment block located near the Max Muay Thai Stadium.

Stepping into the living room after his mother, Sanit announces, "I'll sleep on the couch, *Mae.*" While his mother moves to a wall to tap on the fan switch, Sanit slips his knapsack off his back and puts it on the floor beside the couch. He sinks down in the couch and scans his surroundings.

Ratree gets the strap of her handbag off her shoulder and strides towards her room. "Go help yourself to a cold drink from the fridge in the kitchen." She opens the door and tosses her handbag on her bed.

In the kitchen, Sanit takes out a can of Sting, sits at the dining table and pops the lid. He tilts his head backward, takes a gulp and, as he puts the can down on the table, he notices a round pulp-board drink coaster lying under a squeeze bottle of chili sauce. Its border is emblazoned with the words "Kitson Go-Go Bar" in red. *Huh? Kitson Go-Go Bar?* He picks up the squeeze bottle and looks at the drink coaster. *What's this thing doing here?* He replaces he squeeze bottle on top of the coaster.

After finishing his energy drink, Sanit goes to the living room to join his mother. "Let me show you my term results, *Mae*," he says, reaching for his knapsack. "Tomorrow, can I go see the restaurant you work in?" He unzips the knapsack, pulls out a sheet of paper and hands it to his mother.

"I've taken leave for three days so I can cook for you." Ratree takes the paper and looks at it. "So, I'd rather not go there for a change."

Sanit's eyes scan the living room. "What about the stall at Thepprasit Road?" His gaze rests on the glass ash tray in the centre of the coffee table. *What! There's another Kitson Go-Go Bar drink coaster under the ash tray.*

"Come on, son, let me de-stress for a few days, okay?"

A muffled musical ring tone comes from the bedroom. Ratree tosses the paper on the coffee table, goes inside her bedroom and shuts the door behind her.

What's so secretive about an in-coming phone call? Brows crimped in curiosity, Sanit pads silently from the couch to the bedroom door and puts his ear against it. As he catches bits and pieces of what his mother is saying, a haze of heat crawls up the back of his neck. *No! It can't be true! She's in that profession.*

Three years later ...

Kwanjai and Sanit enter the dining room and the former greets her mother with a hug. "*Mae*, this is my boyfriend," she says, pulling out a chair at the dining table.

Mrs. Wichit beams Sanit a smile and takes her place at the dining table.

Sanit gently lifts a chair away from the table. "Hello, Mrs. Wichit." As he settles himself down on the chair, his manner respectful, Mr. Wichit, seated at the far end of the table, studies him.

"*Phx* [Papa], this is Sanit." Kwanjai tosses her gaze at her father. "We met while we were in university. He's an economics graduate, works as a management trainee in a big supermarket chain."

"Nice to meet you, Mr. Wichit."

"Come, help yourself – don't be shy." Mr. Wichit casts his gaze over the sumptuous dishes on the dining table. "Where do you live?"

Sanit lifts up his fork and spoon "I'm renting a room near my office."

"Where's your office?"

"Asok Montri Road."

"Good, that's in the Central Business District." Mr. Wichit nods in apparent approval. "What about your family?"

Sanit's gut constricts. *Where am I going to hide my face if I tell him the truth?* "Err, I don't have a family." He spears a piece of lemon chicken and brings it to his plate.

Mr. Wichit arches his eyebrows in surprise. "What do you mean?" He tosses his gaze at his daughter for a moment. "Then who paid for your education?"

"My father died of dengue when I was young; my mother was a teacher but she was killed in a road accident during my last year in high school." A spasm jerks in Sanit's jaw. "Luckily for me, she had personal accident insurance." He takes in a deep breath and exhales through his mouth to dispel his discomfort.

"Oh, the poor woman," exclaims Mrs. Wichit. "I'm so sorry."

"*Nan khux reuxngraw khxng chan,*" says Ratree, garbed in a lime-green tunic and baggy pants.

She is sitting on her bed in a ward in Wat Phra Bat Nam Phu in Lop Buri, 150 kilometres north of Bangkok. Nicknamed The Temple of Death, it houses more than one thousand AIDS/HIV+ patients. Ratree's cheeks are sunken and her arms and legs are like bamboo poles. Rows of beds filled with emaciated patients surround her, and a monk, draped in a saffron robe, is shuffling in sandals along a passage between rows of beds.

Her mouth tightened into a hard line, Ratree pauses to look at me with fish-like eyes and then continues to talk to my tourist-guide-cum-interpret and he says, "After Sanit graduated, he changed his handphone number and abandoned me. He was ashamed that I was a bargirl. Later, I found out from his former class-mate that he had married a girl from a rich and respectable family. Subsequently, I became sick frequently and a blood test revealed my condition. So I returned to Bangkok and eventually ended up here."

"Do you feel bitter towards your son?" I say to my guide who interprets into Thai language.

Ratree replies through my interpreter, "No, I still love him, and I forgive him for what he has done; I hope he will be happy with his wife. By providing him with a good education, I know I've accumulated good merits, which will help me have a better reincarnated life." Her face is void of any expression but tears start to mist my eyes.

* * *

Forehead dotted with sweat, Anurak taps the electronic betting screen in front of him. He and five other gamblers are sitting in a circle in the electronic roulette section of Saamnang Resort & Casino (not its real name) in the border town of Poipet, Cambodia. In the centre of the circle stands an electronic roulette wheel.

A recorded woman's voice says, "Five, four, three, two, one! No more bets!" A sign "No More Bets" flashes on all betting screens. A puff of air blows the ball out of its pocket into the roulette wheel. "Six! Six! Six!" one of the gamblers shouts. After the ball circles the wheel several times, it drops into a black pocket. "The winning number is twenty!" says the same female voice.

I've lost again! Anurak's heart leaps to his throat. *I'm wiped out! This is the end of the road for me!* He lumbers out of the hotel and the setting sun casts his shadow long on National Highway 5. His legs, weak from anxiety, carry him to the Canadia Bank and at its ATM, he uses his credit card to withdraw what little cash is left of his credit limit. *It's best for me to leave this world, but let me have a last fling.*

Next, he goes to Poltok Pharmacy at Kbal Spean Village.

"Can I help you, sir?" asks a tanned man garbed in a short-sleeved white overall over a long-sleeved shirt.

Anurak leans on the glass counter. "Viagra."

"You've a prescription?"

"No."

"In that case, I recommend an imitation from China." He shows a thumb-up. "It's as good as the original, and only half the price."

"Sure."

The pharmacist slides open the door of a glass cabinet behind him, takes out a box and picks out a strip of blister pack. "Anything else you need, sir?" He slides the glass door shut and turns to face Anurak. "Err, what about condoms? We've studded condoms, dotted condoms, ribbed condoms and super-thin condoms."

Anurak shakes his head. *To hell with condoms! This will be my last fling, so who needs condoms?*

Minutes later, he is strolling along the driveway that leads to the front porch of his hotel. Midway, a tuk-tuk driver strides forward from his parked vehicle and accosts him. "Mister, you want girls?"

Anurak waves his hand. *Yes I do, but I want a high-class girl not one in those filthy tin shacks.* "*Minmen now yb nih te* [not tonight]."

Stepping into the hotel lobby, he approaches the bell boy hovering near the front desk. "Can you get two casino girls to come to my room?" His voice is a half-whisper. "I want a threesome. Overnight, raw sex. I'll pay you tip."

The bell boy moves away from the front desk. "When? What time?"

Anurak moves in step with him "Tonight, two hours' time." He looks at his wrist watch. "10 p.m."

"Sure, but they're more expensive than outside girls."

"Price is no problem, but how will I know they're casino girls?'

"They will come in their uniforms." His furtive eyes dart from side to side. "But you've to wait until their shift is over. So they may be late."

Nimol, the bell hop, goes to the men's toilet in the lobby and enters a cubicle. With a flick of his wrist, he lowers the lid over the toilet bowl. Raising himself on his soles of his feet, he plunks his butt on the toilet tank and swings both feet to rest them on the lid. He takes out his mobile phone from his trouser pocket and dials a number. "Punthea, where are you now?" He pauses. "Listen, can you lend me two of your uniforms?" He bites his lower lip. "Now! There's an opportunity to make some money. Of course, I'll pay you a big tip." Another pause. "Sure, I'll get them washed before returning them to you. Hmmm …yes, I'm still at the hotel. Okay, call me when you're here."

Rithisak, the owner of a brothel, in the town's red-light district, jabs the answer button on his mobile phone. "Hello? Yes, Nimol." He sits upright in his rattan chair, which creaks. "You've a customer at your hotel?" He wipes his sweat-beaded forehead with his short sleeve. "He wants sex without condom? Sure …no problem. A few of my girls are already HIV positive. They can do anything and everything." He crosses his right foot over his left knee and starts to shake the former, his dirt-caked slipper dangling from his toes. "Hmm …I see … I see …" He ends the call and rises from his rattan chair. "Tssssk!" His hand slips inside his khaki shorts and scratches a raised itchy bump. *Oh shit! I've bitten by a bed bug again!*

Rithisak shuffles out of his room to the hall where a dozen girls are sitting on wooden benches and watching TV. Most of them are in their early twenties. From a rusty metal bracket outfitted in a wooden pillar, a fan groans as it turns slowly, stirring hot air around.

"Mali and Rota!" Rithisak picks up a notebook from his trouser pocket and a stubby pencil wedged behind his ear.

"Yes, *Ba*?" answers a broad-nosed girl of about twenty years old.

He flips to a certain page in his notebook and makes a record of the two girls' business. "Go and bathe, got overnight booking." He replaces his notebook back in his trouser pocket and wedges his pencil behind his ear.

The broad-nosed girl and another girl, her forehead peppered with acne, leap off the bench and saunter to the bathroom. "Hey," says Rithisak, pointing at their feet as they pass by him, "don't forget to put on shoes, not those Japanese slippers."

Half an hour later, the duo boards a tuk-tuk for Saamnang Resort & Casino. Before the vehicle rumbles away, Rithisak re-briefs his girls, "Remember, my agent will be waiting in the lobby. He'll give you casino uniforms and take you somewhere to change into them. Tell the client that you're casino workers, okay?"

Lying on a pillow propped up against the headboard, Anurak is one of the patients in the men's ward of Wat Phra Bat Nam Phu. Minutes ago, after talking with Ratree, I visited the Life Museum in the temple complex, which contains the mummified bodies of AIDS victims before coming here to chat with Anurak. About thirty years old, he has big eyes sunken deep in his head, which sports a crew cut.

Anurak raises both hands to the height of his shoulders for a second. "See the keloid scars of the slash wounds on my wrists?" he says through my guide-cum-interpreter. "I wanted to end my life after my fling. One of the Cambodian girls left her handphone in my room and, a few hours later, she came back to retrieve it but I didn't open the door. She told this to the bellboy. I don't know what happened after that but later someone used the spare key to open my room. They found me unconscious and my bed was soaked in blood. When I woke up, I was in a hospital. Two days later, my parents came and took me back to Bangkok." His fingers tremble as he grips the side rails of his bed. "They paid part of my debts and got a monk to counsel me. The holy man stressed that the Buddhist precept of not killing extends to not even killing oneself. Months later, I started having symptoms and a blood test showed that I'd contracted HIV because of my last romp with those Cambodian sex workers." His eyes fuse to the ceiling in a glazed stare. "So I decided to come here to die."

* * *

Lying naked on her side, Penchan traces the outline of Duncan's face, his cheekbones and his jaw. "Darling, since, you want me to stop working in this line, I need a means to support myself. So, either you send me a monthly allowance or give me money to start a restaurant. I'm a good cook. Then, later, when business is good, I can employ you as manager of the restaurant. In that way, you can get a work permit easily, and can stay in Bangkok for long term. That's what many *farangs* have done."

Duncan gently grasps her fingers and kisses them. "That's a good idea." He rolls over Penchan and crouches on all fours. "But, how much do you love me?"

Duncan MacNeill (a pseudonym), a thirty-year-old divorcee from Glasgow, Scotland, is employed as a plumber in a heating-and-plumbing company back home. Penchan, twenty years old, works as a bargirl in Harlot Pub in Patpong. They first met when Duncan was on a one-month Christmas vacation in Bangkok last year.

Penchan strokes the back of his head. "To prove my love for you, darling, I'll take you to meet my parents. You can tell them your future plans for us and discuss the *sinsod* and other related matters."

Duncan squishes his brows. "What's *sinsod*?"

"That's dowry, an important aspect of Thai culture." She raises her head to brush her lips against his. "We can take a bus to my native village in Roi Et Province. "Tomorrow, I can go buy the tickets and we can leave the following day. The bus journey will take about seven hours."

The previous year, Duncan's first night with Penchan had been memorable. After paying a bar fine to the mamasan of Harlot Pub, he took her to a love motel. The next morning, he woke up with a full bladder and tottered to the toilet bowl. Standing at the toilet bowl, he yanked down his pajama trousers and cast his gaze below. A red ribbon was tied around his willy into a bow. *Oh blimey! She knows the lyrics of The Drunken Scotman! What a smart girl with a sense of humour!* That incident made Duncan besotted with Penchan, and since returning home, he has been chatting regularly with her over his laptop webcam. Tonight marks his third visit to Bangkok within a year.

Duncan lifts up the cup of lemongrass tea and takes a sip. Its lemony-minty flavour sends a pleasant jolt to his taste buds. He puts the cup down on the rattan table. Sitting around the table are Penchan and her parents. The trio makes small talk through Penchan acting as interpreter, and a while later, Duncan segues to the purpose of his visit. "Mr. and Mrs. Sukbunsung, I love your daughter" – he leans forward in his chair – "and she feels the same way about me. Therefore, I want to marry her. May I know much *sinsod* do you want?"

Mrs. Sukbunsung, a fat woman, says something in Thai to Penchan who interprets,

"There's more to just *sinsod*, Mr. MacNeill. First, a blessing ceremony by monks is required, followed by a full wedding dinner, and other obligations as her husband for her security." Penchan leans to wave away a few fat flies flitting around the coconut dumplings and fish cakes sitting on a wooden platter in the centre of the coffee table.

Duncan nods. "Of course, I understand."

"For *sinsod*, we want four hundred thousand baht. As Penchan is among the prettiest girls in Bangkok, we feel this is not an unreasonable sum. Second, payment for monks to perform the blessing ceremony will come to around fifty thousand. Next, the wedding dinner. It has to be held here, of course. As you know, this is a small village where everybody knows each other. So we plan to invite five hundred guests. That will come to two hundred thousand baht. You'll also have to budget something for your honeymoon. Finally, you'll need to buy a matrimonial home."

Duncan blinks as heat swarms his cheeks. *Gosh! Penchan is rather expensive!* He forces a feeble smile. "I'm agreeable to your requests, Mrs.Sukbunsung," – he sucks in a fortifying breath – "but I need time to come up with the funds. Most likely, I'll have to sell my home and car back home." He shifts uncomfortably in his seat. "So, can we take things one step at a time?"

Mr. Sukbunsung, a scrawny man, chips in before his wife can reply, "Of course, a wedding needs careful planning."

Penchan adds in English and then in Thai, "*Mae*, maybe

Duncan and I can go through the religious ceremony first? I'm sure it'll make him very happy." She beams a smile at Duncan. "Darling, we can do it when we get back to Bangkok."

Garbed in traditional Thai clothes, Penchan and Duncan are sitting on the floor in the hall of a temple in Bangkok. Their hands are clasped together in front. Across them, three senior monks are sitting cross-legged on a dais, their palms in prayer position, and they are chanting mantras. From incense sticks planted in a copper urn, white smoke curls upward, a heavenly scent to Penchan.

From the corner of her eye, Penchan casts a momentary gaze at Duncan. His eyes are closed and his face is aglow with happiness. Penchan shuts her eyes, her ears hearing the mantras but not listening. *Poor sucker! This blessing ceremony has no legal validity.* She staves off a grin with a firm clamp of her ruby-red lips.

Earlier, upon arrival at the temple, she and Duncan presented three food baskets to the senior monks. A donation placed in an envelope was included among the items in each basket.

Soon, the two monks finish chanting the mantras and Duncan and Penchan get on their knees to bow three times to them. One of the monks dips a bunch of bamboo strips into a copper container filled with holy water. With two flicks of his wrist, he sprinkles the holy water on Duncan and Penchan.

A fellow bargirl from Harlot Pub has recorded the ceremony using the video function of her smartphone, and the recording would be given to a happy Duncan.

A week later, he rents a two-room flat in Din Daeng district for Penchan and, upon returning to Glasgow, he withdraws his life savings for her to start a restaurant called Wonder Siam.

Three months pass ...

A shaft of sunlight is pouring in through the open window of Duncan's room and, outside, two songbirds perched on the branch of an apple tree are chirping. Duncan leans forward in his chair, staring at the video image of Penchan on the screen of his laptop.

"Sakchai," says Penchan, "please say hello to Duncan."

A broad-faced man moves beside Penchan. "Hello, Duncan." He waves his right hand. "How's the weather in Scotland?"

"It's summer now and the temperate is averaging about seventeen degrees."

Earlier, Penchan told Duncan by email that her brother Sakchai would be coming to Bangkok to look for work. Duncan had briefly met Sakchai in Penchan's parents' home and was agreeable to his brother-in-law coming to stay in the spare room.

"Sakchai is trained as a carpenter." Penchan tosses a side glance at her brother. "He attended two interviews within this week."

"Excuse me, Duncan, I'll leave you to talk with my sister." Sakchai moves away from the webcam at the other end.

"Darling, the restaurant is making a loss." Penchan squares her shoulders. "Its latest accounts have to be submitted when I apply for your work permit. You must make the financial figures stronger, and that means giving me more money to put in as capital. If the restaurant doesn't have money to pay your salary, your work permit won't be approved."

"I'll wire some money to you in a few days' time. I'll fly in end of the month and stay for a week – see what can be improved at the restaurant."

"Bye-bye." Penchan purses her lips. "I love you, darling."

Bangkok

The dining room in Penchan's flat is abuzz with chatter as she, Duncan and Sakchai discuss the possible changes to the restaurant's menu and marketing tactics. Using a wooden ladle, Penchan scoops up a plump prawn from a tureen containing tom yum kung into Duncan's soup bowl. "Have more soup, darling. The sourish taste will help you fight the jet lag."

"Coffee works well for me too." Duncan blinks and, using his hands, starts to remove the screw pine leaves wrapped around a piece of chicken.

Sakchai, seated across Duncan, studies the latter with pensive eyes, and his gaze fuses with Penchan's for a moment.

"Let's change the topic." Penchan says. "Sakchai, why don't you tell my husband the good news?"

"Duncan, I've got a job in a furniture factory." Sakchai's eyes flicker up. "But the factory is very far away. It's inside Warrawut Industrial Estate."

"Darling, can you buy a motorcycle for Sakchai?" Penchan's voice brims with hope. "I think a Kawaski Z125 costs only seventy-five thousand."

Duncan looks up from his plate of white rice, soaked with green curry. "Sure, but I suggest a scooter like the Honda Moove, which is cheaper." He gestures to his brother-in-law. "Sakchai, your petrol bill will be lower for a scooter."

"You're so sweet, darling!" Penchan rewards Duncan with a grateful gaze filled with warmth. "Big bike or small scooter, it does not matter." She lifts her glass of *cha yen* and takes a gulp.

"Thank you, Duncan!" Sakchai performs a deep *wai*. "As long as I've my own transport to get to work on time, I'm happy."

Several days later ...

The glass door of Wonder Siam is locked and a sign "We Are Closed" is hanging from a suction cup hook. Seated at the payment counter inside, Duncan flips open a file marked "Fixed Assets" and scans the documents. *Eh? Why are the prices of the furniture and electrical appliances so expensive? Are these market prices?* He takes out a ball-pen from a pencil holder and jots down the address of the furniture supplier and of the electrical store on a piece of paper. *I think I'll go to these stores and check out their prices.* He gets up from his stool, rounds the counter and goes to the kitchen.

Garbed in a blue apron, Penchan is scooping spice powder using a measuring spoon, while two kitchen helpers are cutting vegetables.

"Darling, I'm going out for a while." Standing in the doorway, Duncan scans the kitchen. "You'll have to man the counter."

Penchan looks up from a row of glass jars containing spice powders. "Sure, I'll be fine."

Fifteen minutes later, Duncan steps out of a taxi into an electrical store.

"Can I help you, sir?" asks a salesgirl, reeking of fragrance from perfume.

Duncan takes out a slip of paper from his shirt pocket and looks at it. "Do you sell the Toshiba Chest Freezer Model CR-A-198M and the Toshiba two-door fridge model GR-A21KPP model?"

"Come this way, sir. I'll show you the products."

The salesgirl walks down an aisle between rows of TVs and washing machines.

She stops in front of a row of refrigerators and chest freezers. "Here you are, sir. The prices shown are fixed and inclusive of delivery."

When Duncan sees their price tags, his jaw drops. *Jesus Christ! Has Penchan inflated the prices or has the store over-charged her?*

His mind in turmoil, Duncan goes to the nearest café, orders a hot coffee and ponders over the situation. Then he takes a taxi to a security supplies store he found on the Internet using his smartphone.

Stepping inside the store, he asks a salesman sitting behind a glass display cabinet, "What type of hidden spy cameras do you have?"

"We've clothes hook, smoke detector, table alarm clock and wall clock."

"Can I see the wall clock?"

The salesman stoops to slide open a door behind the glass display cabinet. "This wall clock is motion-activated and runs on battery." He takes out a round-faced clock about seven inches in diametre and places it on top of the counter for a moment. He flips the clock over, opens the battery compartment and takes out a small chip. "This is the memory card. You can watch the recording on any PC or laptop."

"How long is the recording time?

"About forty hours."

"That's not good enough."

"Then I suggest the advanced model." He points to a wall clock on the bottom shelf in the glass case. "Its memory card is 512 GB. That means sixty hours of recording. It runs on electricity so you've to plug it to a socket."

"Great! I'll take two units." *I'll hang one in the living room and the other at the cashier's counter.*

Three weeks later ...

Duncan gets out of bed in Penchan's room and goes to the washroom to freshen up. Still dressed in pajamas, he opens the door and walks to the kitchen. *Today's the day of reckoning! Time to check the video recording.* He pours some coffee from a pot into a cup, prepares two slices of toast and eats them.

Last month, after having hung the wall clocks, he flew home, and yesterday, he returned to Bangkok. This morning, he told Penchan that he has a headache and wouldn't be going to the restaurant.

He lifts up a kitchen chair and takes it to a spot below the wall clock. Then he stands on the chair and takes the clock off its hook. He flips it over and removes its memory card. After he has replaced the clock on the hook, he goes to sit at the coffee table where his laptop is placed. He switches his laptop on and inserts the memory card, and after a few clicks of the mouse, the video recording begins to play. He presses "fast forward". The scenes in the living room appear routine and normal for a start...

But two hours later, Ducan jerks upright in his seat. In the video, Sakchai is sitting on the armchair and watching TV. A bottle of beer and a mug crowned with a layer of froth are standing on the coffee table. Duncan plays the video at normal speed. A short while later, Penchan, fully naked, walks out of the bedroom and goes to sit on his lap. She wraps her arms around his neck and kisses him. Duncan's mouth parts in shock and his eyes span wider. Penchan and Sakchai speak in Thai for a short while. Then Penchan gets off Sakchai's laps, stands up and leads him by the hand to the couch. She lies down, a smile on her face, and stretches out her arms, ready to swallow Sakchai in an embrace. Sakchai takes off his clothes and makes love to Penchan. The scene hits Duncan like a thunder bolt. His breathing becomes erratic as his mind churns in turmoil. *Damn! Double damn! Sakchai's her husband! What a bampot I've been! The whole family's in this cruel deceit! I better go check the video recording in the restaurant.*

From the kitchen in Wonder Siam, a female worker hears the sound of chairs crashing against tables. She bolts to the dining hall to investigate.

Penchan – her hair in disarray – is grappling with Duncan on the floor. "You bitch!" yells Duncan, his face flushed with anger. "Sakchai's your husband! All the equipment has been bought at inflated prices! You've also pocketed the restaurant's takings!"

Penchan kicks her legs wildly and scratches at Duncan's face.

Duncan gets on his knees, sucks in a harsh breath and raises his right hand. His arm slices through the air as his hand lands on Penchan's cheek.

The female worker hears the thud of flesh against bone and screams, "Call the police! Someone call the police!"

"I was arrested and sentenced to three months' jail for assaulting Penchan who suffered a cut lip and a black eye." Duncan tilts his head and his gaze trails into a faraway look. "The conditions at the Bangkok Hilton – that's the nickname for Bang Kwang Central Prison – were terrible. On the day of my release from prison, I took a tuk-tuk to the restaurant and found that it was closed. I went to Penchan's flat and she was no longer staying there. So I flew home." Duncan sits straight and takes a glug of his beer. "That chapter of my life involving Penchan happened three years ago, but I still come to Thailand for my vacation except that I'm more careful of liaisons with bargirls."

8

Bargirls of Patpong

Ensconced in a hotel room in Patpong, Tony Tan (a pseudonym) from Kuala Lumpur, aged forty, is reading a draft business agreement when he hears a beep of an incoming WeChat message on his smartphone. He puts his pen down on the writing desk and picks up his moby to read the message:

Sawadeekha! I'm college student. My name is Dao. Want short time with me?

Tony's jaw drops when he sees a Thai teenager togged up in a bikini bra in the profile photo and fire starts to lick his loins. She has lively eyes and a round face with high cheekbones.

He replies: *Are you the girl in the photo?*

Of course!

He casts a glance at his watch, which shows 6:20 p.m. *Are you a ladyboy?*

No, I am original girl!

How much? He reckons he has time for a quickie before his dinner appointment with his business associate at 8 p.m.

4000 THB

Too expensive! Give me market price.

3800 THB. Your room number?

Where are you?

Outside the hotel. Your room number?

Tony gives her the room number, puts his smart-phone on the writing desk and walks to the Chubb safe sitting at the bottom of the clothes closet. He opens it and keeps his wallet inside. Five minutes later, the doorbell rings and Tony shuffles in room slippers to open it. Dao, as she appears in her profile photo, steps in and walks round Tony to stand a few feet away. She is dressed in a pair of denim shorts and an off-the-shoulder yellow blouse. A smile lifts the corners of her rose-bud lips. "Hello! I'm Dao."

Closing the door, Tony studies her through wary eyes. "How old are you?"

Dao lifts one foot up and removes her pump shoe with ankle strap. "Eighteen."

She looks pretty young. "Can I see your I.D. card?"

Dao proceeds to remove the other pump shoe. "I've left my I.D. with security downstairs." She locks her gaze with Tony's. "Why you want to see my I.D.?"

"You don't look eighteen."

Her brown eyes plead for understanding. "I swear, I'm eighteen."

Tony hesitates for a moment and releases a sigh of frustration. "Please go, I don't want any trouble with the police." His voice is tinged with caution.

"Please, take me!" She pulls her top over her head, tosses it over her shoulders and throws it to the floor. "I've not paid my college fees last month!" Before Tony can react, she pulls her bra down to her waist to reveal her small breasts.

"Hey!" Tony's eyes become rounder in surprise. "What're you doing?"

She unbuttons her denim shorts and steps out it. "Mister, I need the money badly!" She pulls her panties down to her ankles. "I give you best price – three thousand baht."

"It's not the money. I don't know whether you're under-aged."

Tears start to stream from Dao's eyes and she sinks butt first to the floor, and thrashes her legs like a kid throwing a tantrum. "You sure you don't want me?" Her eyes look up at Tony with self-pity and she starts to sob, her voice choked with emotion. "I need to pay my college fees!"

Tony grabs her wrists with both hands and pulls her up. "Better be safe than sorry!"

"You've seen my naked body!" She stamps her feet. "My future husband has suffered a big loss! You must pay something to me!"

"But I didn't ask you to undress!"

"That's not important! You've seen my naked body. You must pay compensation to me!"

"Okay, okay, anything to get rid of you!" He runs a hand through his thinning hair. "I'll pay you five hundred baht."

"That's not enough." She picks up her blouse and holds it in her hands. "I want one thousand."

"Alright, alright, I'll pay you one thousand." He draws in a calming breath. "Now put on your clothes and leave." He walks to the Chubb safe to get his wallet and the matter is settled amicably.

The next evening, Tony is walking down Soi Cowboy, which is a sea of neon lights from bars and nightclubs. He steps into

Cowgirl Go-Go Bar to check out the quality of the girls. With music blasting in his ears, he moves to the centre stage where several dancers in bikinis are gyrating. His jaw drops. His eyes almost pop. *Great balls of fire! That's Dao! She's a professional go-go dancer! And a damn good actress!* He moves to the edge of stage and glares at her. When she notices him, she blows him a kiss, her lips upturned in a mischievous grin.

* * *

Silver-haired retiree Robert Yap (not his real name), aged 65, from Penang raises his mug of beer. "Cheers!" Sitting across the round metal table opposite him, Sanoh clinks her shooter glass of tequila against the beer mug. "Cheers!" she chugs down her drink and licks her lips. "Darling, want to dance?"

Robert and Sanoh are in a nightclub in Patpong, which is crowded and hazy with smoke. All around them are tables taken up by drunks and bargirls, and they are silhouetted against a brightly lit bar counter at the end of the hall.

"Not tonight." Robert gives a gentle shake of his head. "My legs are tired. I did a walking tour of Chinatown this morning."

"How about supper? You can bar-fine me out and I can be your girlfriend tonight."

"For supper only, yes, but no sex."

"Why?"

"I cannot overdose on the blue pill. I already took one in the afternoon."

"No worries, I can take you to drink snake blood!" Sanoh

kicks off one sandal and rubs her bare foot against his shin. "Darling …It's as good as the blue pill. Then we make boom-boom in your room as many times as possible!" She casts a glance at his wrist watch. "The snake stall in the night market is still open. Come, let's go – it's only fifteen minutes away by taxi."

Minutes later, Robert and Sanoh are walking with linked hands through a warren of hawker stalls in Khlong Toei Market at King Rama IV Road, which is the city's largest wet market. She leads him to a stall with several wire cages filled with cobras. They seat themselves at a plastic table fitted with an umbrella and the hawker comes to take their orders. Sanoh says something in Thai language to him. The hawker nods and goes away. She turns to Robert. "Why don't you go see how the snake blood is prepared?" She shudders her shoulders. "It's gory, I dare not see."

Robert moves to the stall and stands a few feet away. The hawker opens the lid of a mesh-wire cage and grabs a cobra just behind its head, its tail writhing away. He pins the snake on a wooden chopping block and beheads it with a cleaver. The headless body flops for a few moments and remains motionless. The hawker slits its underbelly, removes the still-beating heart and places it on a small saucer. He lowers the bleeding end of the reptile in a glass, allowing the blood to drain into it. From a bottle, he tops up the glass with rice wine. "Your drink is ready, sir," he says, carrying the glass and saucer to Robert's table.

Robert returns to his chair and pays the hawker. He lifts the glass to his lips, tilts his head backwards and glugs down the snake blood. "Phew!" He slams the empty glass on the table and leans forward. "Let's go eat something light, see whether this thing works or not." He rises from his chair. "I prefer a place that's clean and air-conditioned."

Minutes later, they are sitting in a nearby restaurant called Vietnamese and More. After snacking on pork spring rolls and sipping Vietnamese coffee spiked with amarula, Sanoh asks, "Any feeling?"

"Yes, slight but not strong enough." Robert clucks his tongue and cocks his head in thought for a moment. "I better drink another glass of snake blood. Then we can go to my hotel."

"Yipeeee!" Joy curves Sanoh's mouth into a smile.

Hours later, inside Robert's hotel room, Sanoh awakes to gurgling sounds, gets out of bed and switches on the lights. She tosses her gaze at Robert, dressed in pajamas, who is lying face-up, and the air in her throat thickens with shock. His Adam's apple is bobbing up and down and his nostrils are rimmed with blood. *Iiiii! He's choking on his own blood from a nose bleed!* She grabs his shoulder and shakes him. "Robert! Robert! Get up!"

Robert awakes with a start and sits up, choking and sputtering. He leans sideway over the edge of the bed and spits out blood. He looks around as if in a daze, and wipes his mouth with his pajama shirt sleeve.

"*Heoi!* Your nostrils are pouring blood!" Sanoh darts to the dresser table, plucks off several sheets of facial tissues from a box and hands them to Robert. "Shall I call a doctor?"

"No, I need a Chinese traditional doctor." Robert grabs the tissues and holds them to his nose. "Dammit! I've also got a terrible headache."

Presently, Sanoh takes a sip of her Ovaltine Swiss and leans back in her chair. "We took a taxi to the Hua Chiew Hospital in Chinatown. It's opened twenty-four hours." She picks up a French fry and nibbles at it. "Robert was given acupuncture treatment and his nose bleed stopped. He drank too much snake blood, which caused heatiness in his body."

"Why didn't you stop him when he wanted a second glass?" I lean back in my chair and cross my arms.

Sanoh and I are sitting in a MacDonald's restaurant in Soi 4. Her club closed an hour ago and I persuaded her to chat with me for a token payment. She is dressed in slacks and a long-sleeved blouse. A leather bag containing her working clothes and wedges is placed on the empty seat beside her.

"It all depends on your body. Some people can drink two glasses without any side effects. On the other hand, I've come across people who get an allergic rash just from a mouthful of snake blood."

"Do you always bring patrons to drink snake blood?"

"If they need it." She releases a little-girl giggle. "It's a win-win situation."

* * *

Hom steps naked out of the bathroom and goes to the side table of her bed to pick up her mobile phone. Earlier, while taking a shower, she heard its music ringtone blare until it stopped. She sees her friend's name on the missed-call log and dials back.

"What's up?" She moves to the dresser and drags out a chair.

"Hello, Hom? Are you free tomorrow evening? Got opportunity to earn some money."

"Yes, it's my off-day." Hom sits down on the dresser chair and looks at herself in the mirror. "What money-making opportunity is it?"

"The organizer of a naked sushi dinner needs an urgent replacement for their girl. She's down with fever and running nose. The job is easy. Just lie naked on a table, and a chef will put pieces of sushi all over your body. The clients are a bunch of Japanese. They'll eat the sushi off your body. That's all."

Hom cradles the mobile phone between her ear and shoulder. "Where? In a restaurant?" She starts to ruffle her wet hair with her left hand.

"No, in a hotel suite in Silom. The organizer has booked it already."

In the mirror's reflection of herself, Hom sees a twenty-something girl with a long face. "Time of dinner?"

"I'll give the organizer's contact number. Call him and he'll give you the details. His name's Mr. Narong."

Standing in the lobby of a hotel in Silom Road, Hom opens her handbag, takes out her mobile phone and dials a number. "Hello? I am Hom. I'm in the lobby."

"My assistant Kosum will bring you up."

Five minutes later, Hom is ushered into the hotel's executive suite. "I'm Narong," says a slim man to Hom as she performs a *wai*. "Let me show you the dining room." Taking long strides, he crosses the living area to an adjacent room and opens the door halfway to reveal a long polished table with six chairs. "That's the table you'll be lying on." Hom nods, and Narong moves to the kitchen. "This is Mr. Tekeru, our chef." Mr. Tekeru, sporting a crew cut, looks up from the chopping board and casts his gaze down again.

Narong turns to Hom. "Alright, I need you to take a shower, shave off all hair from your body. All the toiletries you need are in the bathroom. Wait in the bedroom until I call for you." He dips his hand into his right trouser pocket and takes out an envelope. "As agreed, here's your advance payment. Kosum will pass you your yukata." He starts to walk toward the living room. "Now, I've to be in the lobby to receive my guests and bring them up." At the door, he throws a backward glance at Hom. "Remember, greet them with *konbanwa*, just do what I've briefed you."

Her feet shod in Japanese slippers, Hom eases the bedroom door open and starts to pad to the dining room. Inside, the lights are switched off except for a standing table lamp in a corner. The moment Hom steps to a few feet from the dining table, Narong flips a wall switch and the chandelier hanging above lights up, illuminating the room to reveal six Japanese men sitting on chairs arranged in a row against one wall. At the same time, Kosum presses a button on a portable mini compo, which starts to play traditional Japanese music, and she moves to Hom's side.

Hom bows in the direction of the diners-to-be. "*Konbanwa!*" She stretches her arms and Kosum unties the bowknot of her sash. Next, she unfurls the yukata and with a flourish, takes it off.

A chorus of "ooooh" and "aaaaah" bubbles from the group

as they gawp at Hom's naked body.

Hom steps up to a square ottoman placed at one end of the table, climbs up the table and lies on her back. She rests her head on a tatami pillow.

The door swings open again and Narong announces, "Gentlemen, I present Chef Tekeru from Osaka!" He claps his hands, which coaxes the dinner guests to applaud, and goes to sit at a corner.

Accompanied by Kosum, the chef trundles a trolley in. It is filled with platters of sashimi, temaki, maki and nigri and a pile of square pieces of banana leaves. After spreading the banana leaves on Hom's body and thighs, Mr. Tekeru begins to transfer the food over with a pair of chopsticks. At the same time, Kosom starts to arrange small plates, sake glasses and chopsticks on the table. The process takes only three minutes. "Gentlemen, dinner is served!" Mr. Tekeru announces and he takes his leave.

The Japanese men go settle at the dining table. There are three chairs at each side to the table but one drags one chair to seat himself at one end of the table. He is facing Hom's legs, which are spread apart, his bulging eyes transfixed on her girl-parts.

The six men start to eat with chopsticks. Slowly, as more and more sake is consumed, their level of drunkenness increases. At a particular point in their meal, they dispense with the chopsticks and resort to picking up the sushi pieces with their mouths. Two men run their tongues down Hom's left and right thighs. Someone pours a dribble of sake on her belly and slurps it up. Another person is nibbling her left breast!

Hom soon realizes that she is on the menu for dessert.

* * *

The lift in the lobby of the four-star Maichai Riverside Hotel (not its real name) arrives at the ground-level lobby with a ding and its twin doors slide open. From inside the lift, Paitoon leans forward to trundle his trolley out into the lobby after having delivered some fresh flowers to the management office of the hotel. He is wearing a pair of sunglasses and his hair is combed backward, accentuating his receding hairline.

As he is crossing the lobby to the main entrance, a woman, about late twenties, enters. She is dressed in an expensive-looking pantsuit and her feet are shod in gold leather flats. A pair of ruby stud earrings sparkles like stars from her earlobes. Paitoon stops a few feet away from her and calls, "Kamlai! Hey, Kamlai!"

The woman turns her head. "Sorry, I think you've mistaken me for someone else."

"Come on, you can't recognize me?" Paitoon whips off his sunglasses. "It's me, Paitoon! "I've opened a flower shop after quitting my bartender job last year."

Ignoring the man, the woman continues to walk to the lift foyer and jabs a button.

Paitoon continues his way out, the wheels of his trolley squeaking, and casts a backward glance at the woman.

Inside the lift, Kamlai jabs the "5" button and it whooshes up.

Oh Lord Buddha, I hope I don't bump into Paitoon again. That fellow looks so haggard. I guess he should be in his early forties now but he looks like an old man of fifty- something.

The lift arrives on the fifth floor and Kamlai gets out. Her heels click on the shiny marble floor as she walks down a corridor past a convenience store and a gym before entering Malee Beauty Spa.

"Good morning, Mrs. Suttirat," greets the receptionist.

Kamlai nods and heads to her office, a cubicle behind the reception counter.

A few days later ...

Kamlai enters the lobby of Maichai Riverside Hotel, makes a beeline for the lift foyer and presses a button. She enters the lift and takes up a position with her back to the wall. The doors slide shut. From behind a pillar in the lobby, Paitoon steps out and takes long strides to the lift foyer. His eyes stare at the lighted numerals at the top of the shut doorway. The lift stops at the fifth floor as indicated by the numeral "5". Paitoon presses the downward-pointing arrow. When the lift arrives, he gets in and jabs "5" on the wall panel. When the lift stops, he gets out and walks down the corridor. He enters the convenience store but does not see Kamlai. Then he goes to the gym, pops his head in the doorway and sees a few hotel guests exercising. *Kamlai is not here either. So, that leaves Malee Beauty Spa. From the way she is dressed, she must be either owner or co-owner of that beauty spa. Wow, she has made a big jump since her days in Patpong.*

A week passes ...

The telephone on Kamlai's office desk rings and she answers it.

"Mrs. Suttirat," her receptionist says, "call from a Mr.

Paitoon." *Click.*

"Hello? How can I help you?"

"Come on Kamlai, er, Mrs. Suttirat, I mean. Why are you avoiding an old friend?"

"Mister, I don't know who you are. Stop bothering me."

"Stop the pretend game. The Kamlai I knew in Winchester Go-Go Bar five years ago never told me she had a twin sister!" Poitoon releases a guffaw.

Kamlai's throat goes dry. "What do you want?"

"My flower business is slack this period. I'd appreciate some support from you." Paitoon harrumphs. "Otherwise your husband may know about your past."

"That's blackmail. And you've no proof at all."

"Remember that Christmas party when our fatty boss dressed up as Santa Claus? There was a group photo of all the bargirls dressed as santarinas. Mamasan Agun still has that group photo and she gave me a copy yesterday. I'm not lying – she's still working in Winchester. I already know where you stay. I also know where your husband works. He's in a respectable profession."

"You've been following me, haven't you?'

"I want four hundred thousand."

"I don't have so much. Two hundred thousand is what I can afford."

"Three hundred thousand."

"Alright. Then you leave me alone, okay?"

"Of course."

"Give me your bank account number and I'll bank it in for you."

"No, I want cash." He pauses for emphasis. "Now listen carefully. You get the cash ready and wait for me at Old Siam Plaza, ground floor. That's where the food stalls are. Is Friday, 2 pm okay with you?"

"Yes."

Carrying a wicker handbag, Paitoon strides to the front glass door of this flower store, unlocks it and enters. He locks the door and hangs a "closed" sign on the suction cup.

Earlier, Kamlai met him at the ground floor of the shopping mall and handed him the wicker handbag. She explained that it contained small notes as they were the proceeds from the spa.

Paitoon places the wicker handbag on his desk and releases the twin clasp fasteners. He opens the wicker handbag and, in the next instant, he releases a gurgled scream, "Aarrrrgh!" A cobra – its hood expanded – rears its head up and lunges forward to spit at him.

"After Paitoon called me, I went to see Mamasan Agun." Kamlai tilts her head backward to glug down her lady's drink. "She denied having given any photo to Paitoon, so I thought he was lying." She squints and pauses as a shaft of strobe light passes over our table. "That's why I put the cobra in the rattan handbag – to teach him a lesson. Later, my husband received a print photo of me taken at Winchester Go-Go Bar. Then I realized that it was Mamasan Agun who was the liar." She flicks her long hair backward with a toss of her head. "My husband became very cold toward me."

"How did you get that cobra?"

"From the wet market selling snake blood. I bought it and asked the seller to put it in the basket. I told him I wanted to slaughter the snake myself."

I take a token sip of my Chang beer. "What made you come back to Patpong?"

"In May, 2014, there was a coup d'etat. Curfew was imposed and tourists stopped coming. After three weeks, the curfew was lifted. My spa business was badly affected. I asked my husband for some money as additional capital but he refused to help me. He and I were already leading separate lives. Later, we divorced."

"You want another lady's drink?"

Before Kamlai can answer, the white fluorescent ceiling lights come on and the music stops. A dozen policemen have entered the bar and two of them have stationed themselves at the main door. There are murmurs among the patrons and bargirls. A voice yells something in Thai language.

"It's a police check." Kamlai's voice is nonchalant. "You brought your passport with you?"

"Yes."

"Quickly throw away your drugs if you have any on your body."

"I don't do drugs."

"Then there's nothing to be afraid of."

The policemen go from table to table to check passports and frisk patrons. At a nearby table, a beer-sodden patron – either Japanese or Korean – is protesting loudly in unintelligible English. "Please co-operate," warns a barrel-chested policeman, raising a fist in the man's face. "Otherwise you get Muay Thai boxing!"

The drunken man pipes down immediately and takes out his passport. Soon, I am body-searched and my passport is checked. When the cops leave, I pay Kamlai a tip and call it a night.

* * *

I lean forward on the aluminium round bar table standing on the sidewalk. "Would you marry an old *farang* and murder him to inherit his property?" My gaze holds Som's for a moment, who is sitting across me.

"Of course not!" Som jerks her head backward. "If he treats me well, I will always love him." Her big dark-brown eyes in her round face seem to reflect the colour of the neons at the entrance of the bar. "Why you ask?" She takes a gulp of her lady's drink.

"I know the story of a true murder committed by a Thai woman."

"Tell me the story." Som shakes one of her squat legs which are dangling over the tripod barstool.

The story runs like this ...

In 1996, Anatol (name changed), aged 32, stepped into Horny Horse Pub in Patpong, Bangkok and a Thai lass garbed in a halter top and mini skirt rose from a nearby table and sauntered towards him with a sway of her butt.

"Handsome man," she murmured in accented English. "Can you buy me a drink?"

"Sure." Anatol smiled, leading his new companion by the hand to the bar. "Order anything you want." He swung a leg over a bar stool and plonked himself down on the cushioned seat. "What's your name?"

"Maylada." Her scarlet lips curled sensuously. "Just call me May." She placed one foot on the footrest of the bar stool and raised herself to ease her butt on the cushioned seat. "Where are you from?"

"Poland in Europe." He cast a gaze at the bartender before locking his eyes with May's. "I'm a potato farmer."

Adjusting a spaghetti strap, May leaned slightly to Anatol. "Oh, how interesting! You must tell me about potato farming in Poland." She gestured to the bartender with a tilt of her chin. "Siam Mary!"

"Where're you from, honey?"

"Isaan, a northwest province in the country."

May and Anatol started to chat like old friends ...

In 1997, Anatol and May, aged 27, were married in a Buddhist ceremony and they moved to Poland. When the country's economy saw a downturn a few years later, Anatol sold his farm and moved with his Thai wife to the resort town of Hua Hin, 200 km south of Bangkok, where he bought two bars. A year later, they were blessed with a baby boy. Soon, May began to accumulate debts through her compulsive gambling and, later, had an affair with a Thai man. By 2004, the couple's marriage had broken down and Anatol divorced May after paying off her gambling debts and giving her a divorce settlement. May then moved to live in Petchaburi town.

Sprawled on the on the edge of the Kaeng Krachan National Park, Phetchaburi town is located an hour's drive from Hua Hin, 75 km south. In 2005, the town had a population of only 26,000.

March 2005

In the living room of her Phetchaburi home, May cast her gaze at her two nephews and a cousin – Pongsit, Supol and Apichat (names changed) – seated on rattan chairs across her. Earlier, she had phoned them to come for an important meeting. The overhead ceiling fan spun furiously within the closed doors and windows of the room as May went through the social niceties to break the ice.

After taking her third sip of lemongrass tea, she put the glass down on the coffee table. "Now, let me get to the point." Her voice was as cold as morning dew. "I asked you to come here because I want my ex-husband killed."

The three men – all in their late twenties – jerked upright in their seats.

"What's in it for us?" Pongsit asked, his eyes gleaming with interest.

"All of you will be handsomely rewarded."

Supol put his cigarette to his lips. "How? How are you going to get the money to pay us?" The cigarette danced on his lips as he spoke.

"I will inherit his wealth through our son whom I have custody of. Anatol is coming to visit him on Sunday. Any one has a suggestion how to murder him?"

Apichat extended his forefinger and curled the other three to mimic a handgun. "I can shoot him with a homemade pipe gun. I use it to hunt birds and squirrels."

Supol took a draw on his cigarette. "But what about the body?" He blew smoke upward and then leaned forward to tap ash on an ash tray on the teak table.

May smiled. "Shooting is a great idea. Let's chop up the body, burn the pieces and dispose of them in the Kaeng Krachan National Park."

Pongsit's jaw dropped. "There're tigers living in that national park. The beasts may eat the remains!"

"So be it!" Saliva sputtered from May's mouth and her eyes glinted like broken glass shards. "I'll prepare the charcoal fire." She rose to her feet. "I need an alibi when you all ambush him. So, when he comes here, I'll be away in the market to buy a few things and then I'll go to the park. When you guys have completed the task, carry his body to the park. I'll be waiting there. Tomorrow, let's go find a suitable spot in the park to dispose of the body. We might as well carry a sack of charcoal there."

The three men nodded in agreement.

March, 2005

Apichat sat on the floor behind the wooden screen standing at the end of May's living room and waited. Carved with decorative arabesque motifs, the screen separated the living room from the dining area. On Apichat's lap lay a slam-fire shotgun. He had constructed the weapon from two pieces of steel plumbing pipe and a teak stock. A wooden dowel with a nail formed the firing pin.

Supol and Pongsit hid in the master bedroom, located to the left of the living room. The two men were armed with a crowbar and a bamboo staff.

Soon, Apichat heard the roar of a car engine outside and the crunch of gravel as the vehicle rolled nearer to the front porch. Holding the shotgun with both hands, he got to his feet and snapped in Thai, "The *farang*'s here!"

Moments later, a tattoo on the wooden front door sounded, and a voice called: "May? May? Hello, May?"

The knocking continued for a short while and then the door knob squeaked as it was turned from outside. A man with receding hairline stepped inside the living room and closed the door behind him. He wore khaki pants and a collared T-shirt with abstract prints of elephants.

Apichat stepped out from behind the wooden screen and aimed the pipe gun at the *farang*'s belly. The Thai slammed the barrel backward against the receiver fixed with the firing pin. *Thud!* Nothing happened!

"Dammit!" Apichat's jaw dropped. "Come out, boys! Get him!" He held the weapon by its barrel, raised it above head and charged at the *farang*.

As Apichat got closer, the *farang* lifted his boot to his chest which sent him tumbling backward. Before the *farang* could react further, Supol swung his crowbar sideways to the *farang*'s ribs which connected.

"Uggh!" The *farang* crumpled to one knee, his face twisted in pain.

The next second saw Pongsit hammering a bone-shattering

blow to the back of his head. The *farang* fell face down and more blows handed on his body until he became motionless.

"He's dead," Apichat hissed, rubbing his chest with one hand, as he rose to his feet. "Let's carry the body to the pick-up."

Sitting on a boulder beneath a rain tree, May drew a sharpening stone over the cutting edge of a meat cleaver resting atop a piece of square burlap the size of a handkerchief on her lap. After giving the blade a few strokes, she heard the call of a bird. Quickly, she bundled the cleaver and sharpening stone with the burlap, and transferred the package to the ground. She knew it was a signal from Apichat as had been agreed between them earlier, but, nevertheless she took cover behind a bush to spy who would be coming down the trail that ran past the rain tree.

Moments later, she saw Apichat and Supol carrying something wrapped in a dirty reed floor mat sagging in a hammock slung from a pole carried on their shoulders. She knew that it was the body of her ex-husband. Pongsit was following them behind, his hand holding a big tin of kerosene.

May appeared from behind the bush. "What took all of you so long?"

"Your ex-husband's as heavy as a baby elephant," grunted Apichat.

May pointed to a rectangular bed of charcoal pieces spread on the ground. "Put the body next to the pyre."

Apichat and Supol lowered the body to the ground, and both men released noisy exhales and mopped sweat off their foreheads. Then, together with the help of Pongsit, they unfurled the reed mat to reveal the body of Anatol. Next, they transferred the corpse to a spot next to the charcoal bed and took off its clothes.

May retrieved the burlap bundle, opened it and held up the huge cleaver with one hand. "You guys help to throw the parts to the pyre." She got down on one knee next to the naked corpse. "I'll start with the head first!" She lifted the cleaver high above her head and brought it down on the neck of the corpse. There was a chilling sound of steel cutting through flesh and bone. Blood oozed out from the severed ends of the neck and trickled to the ground.

Apichat picked the head up gingerly and tossed it to the charcoal bed while May continued to chop at the corpse's limbs, one by one. When every dismembered body part and the victim's clothes had been scattered on the pyre, Pongsit poured kerosene on them. "Oh Lord Buddha, may his spirit rest in peace!" He set fire to the kerosene with a cigarette lighter and flames sprang up, which grew higher and higher.

May and the three men stepped back to watch the combustion. After a while,

Apichat's nose twitched and he screwed up his face. One hand flew to his mouth as if trying to suppress the urge to throw up.

May cast a gaze at him. "What's wrong? Are you squeamish?"

"Yucks! The sizzle and odour of human meat being barbecued reminds me of *gai yang* [grilled chicken]!"

May flicked a gaze at her watch. "I'm going home to change my clothes and lodge a police report that my ex-husband's missing. You guys remain here. When the fire dies, scatter the remains in different spots."

In September, 2006, the judge of the Phetchaburi Provincial Court found May, Pongsit, Supol and Apichat guilty of the murder of Anatol. May, who chopped up and barbequed the victim's body, had her death sentence commuted to life imprisonment. Earlier, the victim's parents had been suspicious of their son's disappearance and had hired a Bangkok-based private eye to investigate. The PI found out from mobile-phone records that Anatol had gone to May's home on the day he had disappeared. Subsequent investigations by Thai police led to the arrest of May and her conspirators and the recovery of Anatol's remains in Kaeng Krachan National Park.

Back to the present ...

Som reaches into her top and adjusts a bra strap. "I haven't heard of that story." She gives a gentle shake of her head.

"You're too young to know about that murder."

Som's pudgy hand grabs my beer bottle by the neck. "Do you know the story about the ago-go dancer in Nana Plaza who was barfined out by a *farang* and was murdered? That was in year 2014. Her name's Laxami Manochat and her body was cut into parts and stuffed in a suitcase. Everybody in Patpong knows about this case." She starts to fill my Willibecher. "The suitcase was then thrown in a river outside Bangkok. Through CCTV recordings at Nana Plaza and other sources, police managed to identify the suspect but he had already taken a train and entered your country through Padang Besar. From Malaysia, he had fled to Europe. Three years later, in 2017, with the help of Interpol, the culprit was arrested in Spain."

"I haven't heard of that story."

"You're too old to know." Som's eyes are bright and as sharp as razors. "My story is as true as yours." Her voice is as hard as rocks.

We lock gazes for a few seconds as tension sizzles in the air between us. Feeling the force of her gaze, I say, "Not all bargirls are bad and not all *farangs* are good."

Som smiles and lifts her shot glass. "Cheers!"

9

Hatyai's Night Butterflies

I step out of my hotel in Hatyai's tourist district and stand on the pavement beside a bright street lamp, waiting to be accosted by a tuk-tuk driver or a tout. The headlights of cars and motorcycles are throwing shafts of light on the tarmac road and slicing the darkness of the night.

As my eyes roam the heavily trafficked drag, I recall an episode at Thai immigration earlier in the afternoon. At the border town of Bukit Kayu Hitam, after my passport has been stamped, I parked my car at Zon Duty Free Complex and took a taxi-van for Hatyai. At the Thai immigration checkpoint, soldiers ordered all passengers out of the taxi-van and searched our bags. Sniffer dogs probed the inside of the vehicle, as if searching for hidden explosives. Later, the taxi-van driver explained that Thai police had received intelligence that fifteen Uigher Chinese – who were suspected terrorists – were hiding either in Hatyai or Danok. Therefore, security has been tightened.

Soon, a stocky man walks up to me. "You booking girl? I take you. Come." Probably in his late twenties, he has a broad forehead and a short but strong chin. His hair is parted on the left and his checked shirt is stretched tightly over his barrel chest.

I reply in Hokkien dialect, "You speak Hokkien?"

He nods. "Yes, can." He extends his hand. "My name's

Nakhun."

I grasp his hand and it's slimy. "I want a night tour of the city." I quickly release his hand. "Are you driving taxi or tuk-tuk?"

"Tuk-tuk." His unblinking eyes stare at me like a predator hunting for a prey. "Where you want to go?"

"Can you show me the KTV clubs and massage parlours?"

"*Eh-sai, eh-sai* [of course]."

A price is agreed and I follow him down the dusty road to his tuk-tuk parked further ahead. I get inside the passenger seat in the front cabin and we take off with a rumble, swerving into heavy traffic. Soon, after a few left and right turns, I am travelling down a road with buildings on both sides splashed with neon lights from KTV bars. The drag is choked with vehicles, their engines blatting and puffing exhaust fumes in the night air.

"Slow down, please. Where are we?"

Nakhun turns his head sideways. "This is Channivet Road. Karaoke shops here have many girls from Laos, Cambodia and Myanmar. You can take them back to your hotel."

"How many hotels in Hatyai?"

"Almost two hundred, thanks to sex tourists mainly from Malaysia and Singapore. And, of course, not forgetting the shoppers."

We zig-zag into Channivet Soi 1, Channivet Soi 2 and Channivet Soi 3. These alleys are also sprinkled with karaoke joints. While passing Channivet Soi 2, Nakhun stops for a moment and points out Yaya Karaoke. "That shop has the prettiest girls and is very popular among those-in-the-know." Now, I'm taken to Chaiyakul Uthit Road where more gaudy neon signs tempt lustful men. Outside a few joints, several "bait-girls" are hanging outside on the pavement to lure nameless darlings in.

"Now I show you soapy massage. Almost all joints have standard set-up. The girls are sitting in a fish tank for you to choose."

Soon, we whizz past one hotel after another, housing spas offering massage with happy ending. We stop at a traffic light and Nakhun shifts the gear to free.

He leans back in his seat. "There's another type of massage called ping pong massage. Mostly performed by older massage ladies."

I cast a sideways gaze at him. "What's that?"

"Massage your genitals."

I release a guffaw, which almost drowns the rumble of the tuk-tuk's engine.

"Hey, this is no laughing matter. Some customers say it's painful, and still others claim that it can cure impotency."

"Got gay bars?"

The traffic light turns green.

Nakhun straightens up. "Yes, I can take you to a gay bar." He engages the gear. "You gay?"

As the tuk-tuk moves away, I look ahead and keep mum.

To my surprise, I am taken back to the Channivet area, and we cruise down the adjoining Thaiakran Road. As the tuk-tuk approaches Top Man Pub, Nakhun eases off the gas pedal. The façade of the pub is adorned with white rectangular designs and an awning protrudes from it. Two tables and several chairs are stationed on the pavement under the awning and one of them is taken up with two young men.

"Stop here for a while. I need to pee." Drat! I've forgotten to bring my prostate medication to Hatyai and I'm now having difficulty holding a full bladder.

Inside the pub, the furniture reminds me of a school classroom. There are small rectangular wooden tables and wooden chairs. Only three tables are occupied by patrons and their male hosts. I go to the bar, order a shot of vodka and slam it down my throat. After paying for my drink, I take long strides to the lavatory and stand facing a wall to piss into a urinal bowl half-clogged with moth balls.

While releasing a slow stream, a pair of hands massages my shoulders for a few seconds. Then they slide from my shoulders, down to my body and to my crotch. Suddenly, the two hands begin to fondle my testicles!

"Eeeeek!" Hot blood whooshes to my face. "Go away, please!"

The hands disappear from my view and I hear footfalls as my "prospective lover" leaves the toilet. Heart thumping, I quickly exit the pub and return to the tuk-tuk waiting at the roadside.

I climb into the cabin, plonk myself hurriedly in the passenger seat and its springs squeak a little. "Come, let's continue the tour."

We whizz past Elysium Sauna, located in an alley off Sripoovanart Road. It is housed in a three-storey shophouse, has dark glass doors on the ground floor and a small neon sign that says "Elysium".

"This is a gay sauna. Got rooftop bar, sometimes got

Underwear Night. You want to go inside?"

"No." *I don't want another testicle massage.* "Where to next?"

"You like ladyboy? Hatyai's most famous place for *ah-kua* [ladyboy] is Hansa Plaza. There're all kinds of shows, mostly performed by ladyboys. You want to watch the cabaret show?" I shake my head and he continues, "I can also show you a few *ah-kua* barbershops! Most of the shops are now closed but tomorrow you can come if you want to. Some *ah-kuas* operate barbershops during the day but at night they work in the karaoke bars or as freelancers."

"Back to my hotel, please."

After a short while, the tuk-tuk stops outside my hotel and I fish out my wallet from my pocket to pay Nakhun, who switches on the dome light.

"Boss, tomorrow, I can take you to consult a powerful monk!" Nakhun studies my face with eagle-like eyes. "I see from your facial features that this is your lucky period. This monk can give you accurate four-digit lottery predictions. You just have to give a small donation to the temple. There are also powerful amulets for sale."

"I am Chinese-Muslim," I lie. "I cannot go to temples." I hop down from the cabin and make a beeline to my hotel.

* * *

Michael, aged twenty-nine, of Kuala Lumpur, opens his eyes as the alarm from his mobile phone on the side table beeps, signalling ten in the morning. He reaches out for the moby and cuts off the alarm. Beside him, Chailai is curled up in a fetal position, her back facing him. Her long hair is spread across her pillow and her transparent negligee reveals that she is a curvaceous goddess of sex who's much sought-after in the Channivet district.

"Chailai …Chailai …" Michael pats her on the shoulder. "Get up."

She does not respond and, seconds later, Michael grabs one shoulder and turns her face-up. Her eyes remain closed and Michael slaps her gently on the face. Her eyelids twitch slightly but she remains fast asleep. Michael gets up to sit on the bed, his piggy eyes assessing Chailai with concern. *My goodness! What's wrong with her?* He grabs his mobile phone and dials her mamasan's number. There is no reply. He tries again, and his call is again unanswered. On the third attempt, the mamasan answers the call with a sleepy voice.

"Hello? Mummy?" Michael exhales a gush of relief. "I'm Chailai's client. Last night, I booked her out, remember? Something wrong's with her. She's seems to be in some kind of deep sleep."

"There's nothing to worry about. She's just stoned, must have taken her fix. Just let her sleep the effects off and she should be okay."

He bends down and starts to look at the inside of both her elbows. "Are you sure?"

"Yes, this thing has happened before."

Jesus Christ! Several needle scars on the inside of her left elbow. "Why didn't you tell me?"

"I don't interfere in the private lives of my girls."

Michael starts to unbutton his pajama shirt with one hand. "So, what should I do? I've to check out at noon."

"Just pay for an extra day. Stay with her until she gets up."

He slips off his pajama shirt. "What! Why can't I check out and leave her alone to sleep?" He yanks his pajama pants to his knees and steps out of them.

"Mister, if something happens to her while she's alone, you're responsible, you hear!" *Click!* The line goes dead.

"After I changed, I went to the reception to extend my stay another day. Then I went out for brunch and went back to the hotel room. To kill time, I watched TV. Luckily, Chailai woke up five hours later." Michael traces a line down his frosted beer mug. "I made her check that all her belongings were still in her handbag before I left. She was apologetic. In hindsight, her Mummy was right. If I had left Chailai alone and someone entered the room and harmed her, I would have gotten the blame." He takes a glug of his beer. "Driving back to Kuala Lumpur late wasn't a big problem for me as I'm a bachelor."

* * *

Salt-and-pepper-haired Songkarn, a retired teacher-turned-translator and petition writer, looks up from his wooden desk, which is tucked in a partitioned cubicle that shares space with a commercial office on the first floor of a shophouse at Thumnoonvithi Road, a short distance from Robinson

Department Store.

Two Thai girls, both about twenty or twenty-one years old, stand at the doorway for a moment and enter. One girl, the taller of the two, is wearing a pair of faded jeans and a beige dress shirt with two top buttons left undone, revealing a pink bra. She has long hair, glossy cherry-red pouting lips and flared nostrils. The other is togged up in jeans-shorts and a crop top that reveals her diamond stud at the belly button. She is slightly plump and her hair is worn as a shaggy bob with bangs over her forehead.

"Yes, how can I help you?" Songkarn gestures to two chairs across him and the two girls sit down.

The long-haired girl sits down and crosses her legs at the knees. "Can you write a letter in English for me?" She places her handbag on her lap.

"To who?"

"My boyfriend."

Songkarn swivels on his chair to face a side table where his computer is placed. He opens a new blank document on the computer screen. "What do you want to say to him?"

"Darling, it's been two weeks since you left Hatyai. But I feel like you've been away for two years." The long-haired girl pauses for a moment to think. "Err ...in my loneliness, I sometimes feel I want to cry. I want you to come back and see me soon. I've not worn the Victoria's Secret lingerie you bought for me. Only your eyes will see my body wearing that sexy lingerie, no one else's. I am yours and will always be yours." She crosses her left arm over her chest and rests the other arm on top of the left hand, placing a forefinger on her cheek to think. "My beloved, yesterday I received a phone call from my mother in my village. My father's water buffalo has died of sickness. The paddy-planting season will start soon. Can you please help my old father? A new water buffalo will cost about one hundred and fifty thousand baht. Can you send me the money as soon as possible? I will always love you. By the way, this letter is written using the services of a translator."

Songkarn clicks the "print" icon and, seconds later, the laserjet printer on his desk spits out the letter. "Here you are." Songkarn places the letter in front of the long-haired girl.

"I also need an envelope." She takes out a name card from her handbag and places it in front of Songkarn. "Here's his address." She picks up the printed letter, folds it twice and slips it inside her handbag.

Songkarn casts his gaze downward on the name card. *Hmmm ... Her boyfriend is managing director of a trading company in Kallang in Singapore. Probably, he's twice her age.* Songkarn writes the name and address on the front of the envelope and flips it over.

"Your name and address, please?"

"Phawta, Snuk Karaoke, Channivet Soi 3, Hatyai."

Songkarn writes the particulars on the envelope and hands it to Phawta who drops it inside her handbag.

The bob-haired girl shifts in her seat. "I also need to have a letter written."

Songkarn flicks his gaze to the computer screen, his fingers of both hands splayed out ready for action. "Please dictate your letter and I'll translate."

The bob-haired girl clears her throat. "My darling, when I

woke up this morning, I was already thinking of you. So first and foremost I want to say I miss you." She scratches the back of her head. "Another week has passed without me seeing your handsome face. Err …My life has changed so much ever since you asked me to be your girlfriend. I am the luckiest woman in the world to have you as my boyfriend. Though you are hundreds of miles away in KL, you are always in my heart." She tosses her gaze to Phawta – who whispers something – and back to Songkarn. "I want to share my joy with you, and I also know that I can depend on you to help me when I have problems. Darling, there are a thousand ways to say I love you but only one way to prove it. That is by action." She flicks a side gaze at Phawta who shows a thumb-up. "Two days ago, my brother phoned me. He said my family's monkey, which plucks coconuts, has died of a terrible disease. For the time being, my mother has replaced the monkey. Every day, she has to climb more than ten trees to pluck coconuts. This is very dangerous work for my mother. Please wire me some money so that my father can buy another monkey. Thirty thousand baht will be sufficient. I look forward to your next trip here. I am yours eternally."

"Those two bargirls are from poor families and have never attended school. So, they don't know how to use the computer and Internet." Songkarn jabs a piece of mango with his fork. "They came here to escape poverty. Phawta was washing dishes in a restaurant, and the other girl was a janitor in a shopping mall." He bites a piece off and starts to chew. "But they did not stay long in their respective jobs because of the low pay, so they became bargirls. After their first visit to me, they've become my regular clients. That's how I know their background."

I take a sip of my *nom yen*. "If they can't speak English, how do they talk with their clients?"

"Either in Hokkien or Teochew. These two dialects are widely spoken in Hatyai. They must have picked up one of these dialects along the way while working here." Songkarn spoons a lump of sticky rice and brings it to his mouth. "And I've noticed that a man who has a Thai girlfriend will eventually learn to speak a little bit of Thai language."

"These stories about water buffalos and coconut-plucking monkeys are just excuses to squeeze money, aren't they?"

Songkarn jerks upright in his wooden stool, his spine becoming as straight as a bullet's path. "We can't choose our parents or the circumstances we're born into. Everybody has to make a living and everyone wants a better life for oneself." His voice is pregnant with stoic impartiality. "I don't judge my clients whatever profession they're in."

* * *

The moment I step into Ying Pub (not its real name) near Lee Gardens Plaza, I am enveloped by live music from a band and swirling cigarette smoke. The walls and floor of the hall are bathed in orange hues from neon lights, and half of the dozen-or-so tables are occupied with patrons and bargirls. At a table in a distant corner, a young bargirl is sitting alone. She is dressed in a T-shirt and blue jeans. Aha! Maybe I can interview her for interesting stories. I stride towards her table, pull out a chair and sit down.

"Hello, what's your name?" I ask in English.

The bargirl flicks her gaze from the band to me and the ghost of a smile shadows her lips. She has a flat-and-wide face and a boy's body, with no waist and a flat chest.

"You speak English?"

She makes a fist with a thumb sticking out, tilts her head and jerks her fist.

I gesture to a waiter crossing the hall. "One lady's drink and one Chang beer – big bottle." I sit up straight in my chair and shoot her a warm smile

She studies me through bright, lively eyes, clasps her hands together and rests them on the table. Her gaze flicks to the band and back to me.

I fire away in Hokkien dialect. "*Lu ha mi mia* [what's your name]?"

She purses her lips as if blowing a kiss.

I cup my ear with one hand and lean forward. "Pardon?" I ask in English.

She remains motionless, as if in a daze.

The same waiter arrives with a shot glass and my beer and sets them in front of me and the bargirl. "Boss," he says as his gaze travels to me, "this bargirl's dumb and deaf. Shall I call Mummy to get a second bargirl to join in?

* * *

"Darling, I've good news for us." Kaipo's lips upturn in a smile.

"I've got a job in Penang. It's a two-year contract. After two years, I can make plans for our future marriage. Would you like to join me there?"

"Sure, if I get a job there." Haimi takes a sip of her soft drink. "I hate to be away from you for too long."

Twenty-three-year-old Haimi and her boyfriend of four months, Kaipo, aged thirty, are sitting in a stall in the Vangthong Night Market at Boulevard Khounboulim, Vientiane, Laos. The boulevard is packed with stalls selling everything from food to handicrafts to souvenirs. Hordes of tourists and locals are bustling past Kaipo's table like ants in a colony.

"That's great!" Kaipo suddenly sits up straight. "I can ask my agency's lady boss." He squishes his eyebrows. "But if you leave, who will help to man your father's stall?"

"That's my parents' problem," Haimi sneers, twisting her lips. "I'm sick of staying in the slums of Thong Khan Kham!"

Kaipo drags his mobile phone of out of his trouser back pocket and dials a number. "Miss Maleah, this is Kaipo speaking. I'm with my girlfriend now. She says she wants to go to Penang with me. You still have any vacancies for women there?" His unblinking eyes brim with hope. "You have? Electronics factory …I see …training provided, that's fantastic. Can you arrange a job for her?" His eyes twinkle with joy. "Yes, yes, your standard agency fee is not a problem."

Two weeks later, Haimi is at the train station at Thana Leng Village seeking out Meleah, the owner of the employment agency. She finds Maleah easily as the latter told the former the colour of her clothes and that she would be waiting at the ticketing booth. Maleah turns out to be a fat woman in her forties with a glum-looking face.

"I've already bought the tickets," Maleah says. "But we've to wait for two other girls." Soon, she is joined by two lasses, whom she introduces as Malu and Palila to Haimi, and that they are also travelling to Penang for their new-found jobs in Bayan Lepas Industrial Park.

Earlier, Kaipo told Haimi that he'll be flying in by a budget airline two days earlier and the air ticket was sponsored by his employer. But Haimi's electronics factory, according to Maleah, did not sponsor any transport from Vientiane to Penang.

At 5:30 p.m. sharp, after clearing immigration, the three girls and their employment agent board the train, which heads to Nong Kha in Thailand. Then they board the overnight train to Bangkok, arriving in Hua Lamphong station at sunrise. Next, Maleah and her charges travel by taxi to Southern Terminal for a quick breakfast before boarding a bus at 7:30 a.m.

After travelling for fourteen hours south from Bangkok, the bus stops at a station and Maleah gets off. She herds the three girls into a taxi, which takes them to a karaoke bar. "Come, let's go in." Maleah pushes the glass door open and steps inside.

"Where are we?" asks Haimi, wheeling her suitcase behind her and looking around her environs. Several tables are taken up with customers and bargirls.

"Girls, please follow me." Meleah leads the three girls to a back room where a scrawny woman is seated at a desk in one corner. The three girls sit around a coffee table and deposit their suitcases on the floor. "Everybody …listen, I've an announcement to make." Maleah flits her gaze across the faces of the three girls. "I got a call from the factory in Penang shortly after we left Bangkok. All their vacancies have been filled. But luckily for all of you, there are vacancies in this karaoke bar. We're now in Hatyai." She pauses to let her message sink in. "In this karaoke bar, your work is to serve the patrons food, drinks and sing songs with them. Anyone who doesn't want the job please refund me the cost of train and bus fares *now*. I'm afraid you've to go back to Vientiane on your own. I'm continuing my journey to Malaysia as I've important business to attend to there." She gestures to the scrawny woman. "Let me introduce Mummy Nathaphon. She's going to be your new boss, okay?"

Alarm seeps into Haimi. "Wait! Let me call my boyfriend first." She takes out her handphone from her handbag and dials Kaipo's number but there's no reply. "Odd, he doesn't answer."

Malu grabs her handphone out of her handbag. "Let me call my boyfriend too!"

She jabs the buttons of her moby repeatedly in frustration. "Bloody hell! His handphone is switched off – that's not his habit – his handphone is always on. Told me he would be flying to Penang yesterday." Her eyes turn moist. "I think that bastard has tricked me!" She pulls out her PVC purse and shows the plastic window, which has a photo of her boyfriend. "Look at this piece of shit! So handsome, yet so devious!"

Haimi's jaw drops. "H-He's your boyfriend? He's also mine!"

Palila lets out a gasp of horror. "He's also my boyfriend!

We've been tricked!"

Back in Vientiane, Kaipo dials a number on his mobile phone. "Boss, the three girls have been delivered. My role's completed." Sitting in a thatch-roofed floating restaurant on the Mekong River, he casts his gaze at the slow-flowing muddy waters but only sees the faces of the three girls. "When can I collect my payment?"

"Good work, Mr. Romeo. I'll check with Maleah tomorrow and you can come to my office the following day."

Kaipo takes a drag at his cigarette. "You want more girls?" As he speaks, white smoke swirls upward from his open mouth.

"Of course! Our Laotian girls are in demand in foreign countries as they're considered exotic."

"That's how I came to Hatyai." Haimi raises the cigarette in her hand to check its length and takes a deep draw. "After three months in my former bar, I got a tattoo drawn on my back and my belly button pierced." She lifts her chin and exhales a stream of cigarette smoke. "This is my fourth month in this karaoke club."

"What happened to the other two girls?"

Haimi is sitting opposite me across a low, black-lacquered coffee table in a nightspot in Thungsao Road. As it is Happy Hours, there is no band yet and the place is brightly lighted.

"One went back to Laos after a couple of months." Haimi crosses her legs at the knees and her mini skirt rides upward, exposing smooth thighs. "I don't know what happened to the other girl but I chose to remain in Hatyai rather than go back."

"Are you happy here?" I hoist my beer stein to my lips.

"At first, I didn't like working here but later, I realized that it has opened a new world for me." She uncrosses her legs, and deliberately holds the other leg high for a moment to expose her crotch to me. "I've more financial freedom."

Great balls of fire! She's not wearing panties! I half-choke on my beer and start to thump my chest with an open palm to stop coughing. "Excuse me, I gotta go." I rise to my feet, my eyes brimmed with tears. "I want to watch the sexy show in The Dome." I take out my wallet, toss some money notes on the table as tip and leave.

The show starts and a troop of tall girls dance about on stage. Flaunting their figure in cropped tops and mini-skirts, they take turns to successively belt out Thai and English numbers. Then, to the pulsating beats of techno music, they remove their tops in slo-mo. Beams of lights chasing each other cross over their bodies, making the star-shaped pasties on their nipples glitter and shine. During this time, three hundred pairs of eyes bulge in their sockets. From the corner of my eye, I spot a nearby fatso, probably in his early twenties, drool saliva out of the side of his mouth.

I am now in The Dome Exclusive Club in Hansa JB Hotel in Jootee Anusom Road. (I don't think "JB" has anything to do with Johor Bahru).

The first segment of the show ends and, moments later, another troupe of dancers prances to the stage. They are garbed in two-piece stripper outfits. As deep bass throbs, sounding like distant thunder, the dancers wriggle slowly like worms and eventually peel off their tops.

"Bah! This second group of girls has smaller breasts compared to the first," sneers a loud voice behind me. "I'll be happy to have one of the earlier girls in my hotel room."

"Hey, are you bonkers?" asks his friend. "The first group consists of ladyboys."

* * *

Thirty-five-year-old Sansuka (a pseudonym), a Ceylonese-Malaysian from Kuala Lumpur, steps out of his hotel and starts to stroll towards Thamanoonvithee Road.

Earlier, he told his wife he's going to browse at a Buddhist amulet store in Odean Fashion Mall and for a drink at a nearby pub. His wife – weary from window shopping – said she preferred to rest in the hotel room.

Sansuka has walked not more than two hundred metres when a girl, probably early twenties, approaches him.

"Hello, handsome man!" Her voice is honey-sweet. "I'm Nut. You want short time?" Her mini-skirt wraps her buttocks tightly like a *bachang* [rice dumpling] and her v-neckline blouse clings to her body loosely, allowing ample views of her round breasts.

Sansuka assesses her through widened eyes. *Wow! She's a stunner. A bit short, probably five feet two only, but she has curves in the right places. Got the voice of an angel. Her facial features are also faultless.*

"How much?"

"Three thousand baht."

I'll try to get best price. "Two thousand."

"No, three thousand but I promise good service. We can do everything: DFK, DATY, 69 and B2B massage. What you pay is what you get. Where's your hotel?"

"We can't go to my hotel. My friend's in my room."

She hikes the strap of her handbag higher up on her shoulder. "We can rent a room nearby."

"No problem, but you pay for it."

"No, you pay for it."

Sansuka shakes his head. "Then I'm not interested."

"In that case, why don't you come to my house?"

"Where?"

"Five minutes' away by walking."

Sansuka considers for a moment. "Can I take your photo?"

"Why?"

"If you have gangsters waiting to rob and kill me, my friend can report you to the police."

Annoyance pinches at Nut's brows. "Don't be silly! Alright, you can take my photo but it will cost another two hundred baht."

"Deal."

Nut shows a V-sign and smiles to reveal neatly arranged teeth as Sansuka clicks her photo with his smartphone. He sends the photo to his buddy with a text message. "Call the police and show them this photo if something happens to me in Hatyai." His heart swells with pride as he shows Nut the sent text message on the screen of his smartphone. "I'm a veteran in this line." He taps the side of his forehead. "Smart, eh?"

Nut slides him a thin smile. Soon, they walk to a nearby shophouse a few blocks away. Nut leads Sansuka up a staircase to the third floor and the former opens the wooden door. A blast of warm stale air hits Sansuka in the face when he steps in. "See, darling, there's no one here." Nut crosses a sparsely furnished hall and enters her bedroom with en-suite bathroom. She switches on the side table lamp and the air-conditioner and starts to undress. "Let's shower, darling."

Sansuka's eyes turn as bulgy as those of a frog. *Oh Lord Buddha, she's Hatyai's smaller version of Pamela Anderson of yesteryears! I've gotten myself a best buy. Whoopee!*

True to her words, the post-shower deed is delivered with extras such as torrid DFK, DATY, 69 and body-to-body massage thrown in. Sansuka, a veteran womanizer, has never been so satisfied in his life. After the deed, they shower again. When Sansuka and Nut step out of the bathroom, she switches on the ceiling lights, which illuminate the room brightly.

Shivering slightly from the cold air, Sansuka strides to grab a cotton towel from the clothes hook behind the door and notices a framed photo on the dresser. "Who's that man?" He towels himself dry. "Your boyfriend?" He picks up his briefs from the clothes hook. "Wow, he's handsome."

"No." Nut slips her arms into her bra straps.

Sansuka steps into his briefs. "Your brother?"

Nut reaches her hands behind her back to fasten her bra. "Nope."

Sansuka takes his pants from the clothes hook and sits on the bed. "Your father?" He slips his feet into his pants and pulls the latter up.

Nut wears her panties. "Don't be silly!" She steps into her

mini skirt, wriggles her big butt into it and hooks the buckle of the skirt.

Sansuka stands up and buttons his pants. "Your husband?"

"Of course, not!" Nut takes her blouse from the clothes hook. "I've told you I'm single."

Sansuka starts to wear his shirt. "Then who's he?"

Nut slips her blouse over her head. "That's me before my sex-change operation."

"Holy cow! Yucks!" Sansuka makes a face. "But – but you're short and petite."

"Darling, there are tall ladyboys and short ladyboys. I was a short man." She releases a little-girl giggle, which bounces off the walls of the room. "You're not that smart after all, darling." She goes to sit at the dresser and starts to comb her hair.

* * *

Leaning on two pillows stacked against the headboard of his bed, Eugene (not his real name), a late-twenties bachelor, is looking at the TV in his hotel room but his eyes are seeing mental images of a Thai girl who's coming soon. *I wonder how she looks like without clothes?* He checks his watch: 9:10 p.m. *Should be here any minute now.*

Outside, raindrops are pattering on the window and sliding down the glass pane like silver beads. The downpour, which started three hours ago, discouraged him from visiting the Channivet area after his tom yum kung dinner in the hotel's restaurant and he sent out a message using his WeChat's "People

Nearby" feature. He wrote: *Lonely Chinese-Malaysian seeking overnight girlfriend. Not more than 25 years old, please.* Within five minutes, he received four replies. From the profile photos, the prettiest girl was Pim, who stated: *My name's Pim, short for Pimchanok. I can be your overnight GF. We meet to discuss?* He replied: *Room 24, Laila Hotel, this is a bachelor's hotel, so you can come up.*

The doorbell rings. He hops down from his bed, slips his feet into slippers and shuffles on the carpet to open the door. Standing in the doorway is Pim, who has a round face, plump lips and a delicate nose. A tote bag is slung from one shoulder, and a wet umbrella dangles from the crook of her left arm. "*Sawadeekha,* darling!" She performs a *wai* with a smile revealing teeth that runs straight but with a small gap.

Eugene steps aside to allow her to come in. "So, how much do you charge?" As he closes the door, he flicks his gaze from her face to her cleavage and his groin suddenly tightens.

Pim stands a few feet away from Eugene. "Four thousand plus five hundred as a bar-fine."

His eyebrows inch up in surprise. "What bar-fine?"

"I'm from the high-class Tigress Bar, two blocks away."

"I don't believe you." Eugene plants his hands on his hips. "You're a freelancer."

"I'm not lying." Pim takes out her smartphone from her tote bag. "Here, you can talk to my Mummy." She dails a number, looks at the screen and thrusts the moby to Eugene.

"Stop this silly game." *Business is slack at the bar because of the rain!* Eugene pushes her hand away. So, *it's time I drive a hard bargain!* "That woman can be anybody – your friend, your mother or your sister."

"Please, talk to her. I told her I was coming to meet you. She released me on condition that I hand over your bar-fine to her."

"Even if it's true you're from Tigress Pub, I didn't go there to book you out. You came here by yourself. And your asking price of four thousand is on the high side." He shows his moby to Pim. "See? I've three other girls are interested to be my girlfriend."

She starts to fold her wet umbrella. "Alright then, payment in advance."

"No, fifty percent now, the balance tomorrow."

Pim leans the umbrella against a wall near the door. "You're a difficult customer to deal with."

Eugene flashes a snide smile. *Bargirls are tricky! Pay in advance and you'll get bad service!* Pim ignores his smile and steps out of her heels.

The next morning, Eugene wakes up and feels his dickie being gripped tight. He blinks a few times and a horrified gasp spews from his mouth.

Clad in a silk negligee, Pim is sitting on the bed and her face is in a scowl. "It's time for me to leave." One of her hands is holding a penknife to Eugene's manhood, which is pulled taut by her other hand. "Are you going to pay the bar-fine with the balance or not? If not, I'm going to cut it off!"

"Y-yes!" Eugene's body goes stiff. "Please, release my dickie!"

10

Kuala Lumpur Potpourri

"Ladies and gentlemen," the middle-aged announcer says, "let me present to you, the dynamic harmonica duo, Ken and Mei, from Hulu Selangor." With a flourish of his arm, the announcer moves away from the standing microphone and disappears into the left side-wing. The patrons in the food court applause and spotlights throw beams on the centre of the stage.

Pimply-faced Ken and his girlfriend Mei, both eighteen years old, step up to the standing microphone. They were the concert winners of their alma mater Phor Thor Independent High School (not its real name) last year. Ken's hair is neatly plastered back with cream and fair-skinned Mei is wearing light make-up and a short puff-sleeved dress. The duo whip out their expensive Hohner-brand harmonicas and start off with classic Chinese romantic songs such as *Qíng Rén De Yǎn Lèi, Ya Lai Xiang, Qiu Tian De Ge* and several others.

After twenty minutes, they take an intermission and snag a table near the stage. They order food and drinks. A while later, Ken is sipping a soft drink when a woman – already in her mid-thirties and garbed in a halter top – approaches him. "*Qin ai de* [dearest]," she says, looping an arm over his shoulders, "you want to be happy?" Her red lips upturn in a smile. "We can play

Nǔshén Kuān Yīn qímǎ!"

"Goddess Kuan Yin rides horse?" Ken scratches his head. "Huh? What's that?"

The woman bends slightly on her knees and whispers in his ear.

"What! That's called Goddess Kuan Yin riding horse?" Ken sputters, his face blanching. "No, no thanks." He pulls out a white cotton handkerchief from his shirt pocket and wipes his forehead, suddenly beaded with sweat.

Seated across Ken, Mei glares at the woman as she moves away. "Who's she?"

Jealousy is written on Mei's face. "The nerve of her!"

Ken shakes his head. "I don't know." His gut cramps.

Recorded music from hidden speakers keeps the entertainment going as Ken and Mei continue to eat their noodles. Shortly, a forty-something drunk, togged up in a light-coloured short-sleeved shirt, steps out of the semi-darkness and approaches Mei. "*Xiaojie* [Miss] I haven't seen you here before, I think you must be new. What's your price?"

Mei turns her head sideways to look at the man and her eyes become rounder from shock. "Huh? What price?" She puts her chopsticks down on the table. "Price for what?" Her voice turns edgy.

"*Zuo ai* [make love]." The man's lecherous eyes caress Mei from her face to her chest, and he puts a hand on the back of her chair.

"Hey, I don't do that! I'm only a harmonica player!" She holds an invisible harmonica to her mouth with both hands to stress her point.

The potential john's smile turns into a grin. "Ah, you only give oral sex! Great! I'm also keen on that! How much?"

Ken rises to his feet on weak knees. "She means we're harmonica performers on stage." He inhales a fortifying breath. "Please, please leave her alone."

"Oh? Really?" The man takes a step backward. "I just arrived. Sorry, I didn't see both of you on the stage earlier."

When the drunk disappears, Ken steps up to the matronly woman manning the nearest hawker stall. "Madam, what kind of place is this? Why are people saying funny things to us?"

"You don't know?" The woman lifts the front of her apron to wipe her face. "This is a red-light food court."

Ken returns to his table where a pale-faced Mei is finishing her noodles. He pulls out his mobile phone and jabs a few numbers. "Hello? Mama? Mei and I are taking the first bus home tomorrow! We're at the wrong place and wrong time!"

* * *

Simon (not his real name), an early-thirties bachelor, stares at his computer screen and jots down the phone numbers of several social escort agencies on a piece of paper. He puts his ball-pen down on the writing desk, picks up his mobile phone and calls the first agency on his list.

"Hello? Ruby Escort? My name's Alex. Do you have any pregnant social escorts?"

"What? Is this some kind of a joke?"

Simon kicks away from the writing desk and leans back in his swivel chair. "No, I'm serious." He places both feet on his writing desk.

"No, we don't."

"In that case, you've any escort who's going to have her period this weekend? I want to book her this coming Saturday, an overnight trip."

"Huh? You sure that's what you want?"

Simon lowers his voice to a serious level. "Yes, I'm very sure."

"Alright, hold the line, I'll ask my girls." There is silence for a long while. "Sir, our Viet Cong doll Bao says her period's expected this Friday through next Monday. You interested?"

Simon jerks upright and places his feet on the carpeted floor. "That's great!"

Shivering from the cold, Simon and Bao step out of the bathroom after a hot shower and quickly dry themselves with cotton towels. Minutes ago, they rattled the wooden bed – almost breaking one of its legs – and Bao's menstrual blood stained the sheets on the mattress.

Simon goes to his small duffel bag and takes out a pair of red panties and a bra of matching colour. "Here, darling, please put these on – they're free size." He hands them over to Bao. "We're going to the casino after dinner." He pulls out a pair of red boxers and steps into them.

Bao releases a guffaw and her breasts quiver like jelly. "Darling, why are we wearing these?"

"Don't you know? A menstruating woman, a pregnant

woman, and red underwear all confer luck on a gambler! That's Chinese belief. So I want you to tell me the numbers to bet on." Simon arches his eyebrows and a hopeful smile stretches across his face. "If I win big tonight, there's a tip for you!"

* * *

The emcee of the graduation ceremony looks down at a piece of paper. "Liza Loh, B.A. in Accounting, Pass Degree." Stationed at a lectern at the side of the stage, he pauses and his gaze scans the students seated in the hall. He sees the recipient-to-be squeezing between two rows of seats, trying to get to the middle aisle.

Liza (not her real name), togged up in mortar board and graduation gown, starts to climb up the steps to the stage. Scores of eyes follow her statuesque figure and gliding long legs as she crosses the stage to accept her scroll from the president of the college.

Kane Kok (not his real name), aged forty-five, is sitting among the audience, using his smartphone to record the occasion. *Dammit! Why didn't she inform me of today's graduation? I only found out from the college's website three days ago!* He switches off the video feature of his smartphone and puts it back into his trouser side pocket.

An hour later, the ceremony ends and the guests and graduates disperse to the outside lobby for refreshments. Kane, togged up in a necktie and smart office attire, leaves the hall and searches for Liza among the crowd. Eventually, he sees her standing with a fellow male graduate near a buffet table. They are sipping coffee.

Her companion is well-built and wears his hair like a mop. His big eyes shine with intelligence and honesty. Kane walks towards Liza.

"Hello, Liza." Lips stretched into a smile, Kane stops a few feet from her. "Congratulations! Can we take a photo together?"

Liza's almond-shaped eyes glare at him, glinting with ire. "Why should I take a photo with you?"

Liza's companion glazes a hard stare at Kane and returns his gaze to Liza. "Who's this guy? You know him?"

"Just ignore him! He's just a piece of shit!"

Kane's ribcage freezes in shock, almost making him unable to expel air. "I'm your boyfriend! And you call me a piece of shit?"

"Please, don't harass me anymore!" Liza scalds him with a look. "Stop your rubbish! I'm not your girlfriend! Never was!"

Liza's companion blinks, annoyance squishing his brows. "Who's he, actually?"

"He's just a loan shark!" Liza's voice is filled with scorn. "I took a loan from him to help pay for my fees. Then he asked me to be his girlfriend. I refused but he's been pestering me with text messages. I've only one final installment to pay. Once I start work next month, I'll be able to make the last payment. Then, I'll have nothing to do with him anymore."

The air in Kane's throat thins. "Loan shark, eh? Now you're showing your true colours! You bloody bitch! I should have known this was too good to be true." His world slows to a stop as his body feels numb and a strange buzzing fills his brain.

"Hussein! Aziz!" Liza's companion flaps his hand in one direction. "Can you boys come here, please!"

Two strapping young men stride towards Liza's companion. "Yo, what's up, buddy?" asks the bigger of the two.

"This guy is harassing Liza. Give me some back-up, please."

Displaying faces that are almost fit for a Maori Haka, the male trio stands in a semi-circle facing Kane. "Mister," grunts Liza's companion between clenched teeth, "please leave my girlfriend alone." He points a menacing finger in his face. "Or we'll call security and throw you out." One of his friends joins in the intimidation. "Yeah, get out, you bloody goat."

One year earlier ...

Kane takes out a small velvet box and hands it over to Liza across the table. "My dearest, Happy Birthday!" He is togged up in a short-sleeved poplin shirt and slim-fit linen trousers.

"Thank you, Kane." Liza takes the velvet box from him and opens it. "Oh, a beautiful gold bracelet and a neck chain!" Her mouth is shaped like a Valentine heart as she smiles and her long hair frames an angular face with high cheekbones.

Kane and Liza are sitting in a French restaurant in the city's Golden Triangle.

Three roses in a vase and a candle in a circular cut-glass holder are standing on the side of the table between them.

Kane takes her left hand and kisses it. "Liza, can you be my second wife after you graduate?"

Liza closes the velvet box. "You mean mistress?" She puts it in her handbag resting on her lap.

"Mistress or second wife, does it make any difference? What's important is that I love you." He flicks his gaze to a bow-tied waiter approaching the table with two bowls in his hands. "Ah, the lobster bisque is here."

The waiter sets down the soup bowls containing orangish-yellow goodness and goes away.

Liza picks up a spoon and her mascared eyes fuses with Ken's for a moment. "Darling, you've been so nice to me. I'll be more than happy to be your second wife." She looks down at her soup and sweeps her eyelashes upward to pin her gaze with Kane again. "And I'll bear you plenty of children!" She takes a sip of her lobster bisque. "Hmmm …this lobster bisque is better than sex!"

An ache of lust suddenly burns in Kane's groin. "Oh … I've booked a room for one full night in Marmalade Hotel. Sorry, I forgot to tell you earlier." He lifts up his spoon to scoop his soup.

Two hours later …
"Eeeeewwwww!" Kane grunts.

"You've come, darling?"

"Hell no, my hips popped!"

"Again?"

"I'm afraid so."

"Roll over, let me massage your hips."

"Please do. Leave the lights off."

In darkness, Liza kneads Kane's hips. "Darling," she whispers after a short while. "I've something to ask from you."

"Yes, dear?"

"Can you buy a car for me?"

"Why, of course!"

Two years earlier ...

Kane Kok looks up from the menu. "I'll order later," he says to the waiter, putting the menu down on the table. He takes out his mobile phone from his trouser pocket and dials a number. "Hello? I'm Kane. I'm in the restaurant now."

"Where's your table?"

"In front of the cashier's counter."

Ten minutes later, Liza enters the café and walks straight to Kane's table.

Her butt is encased in fake-leather hot pants and her hair is tied up in a pony tail.

Kane rises slightly and sits down again, his lips tilt in a warm smile.

She drags out a chair. "Hi, waited long?" Her voice brims with self-confidence.

"Not really." While admiring her sharp flawless features, Kane absentmindedly strays his hands to his necktie to adjust its knot. "Menu." He snaps his fingers at a waiter hovering nearby.

They order food and drinks.

"Your advert says you're looking for a sugar daddy."

Liza crosses her slender legs at the knees. "Yes."

"Can you tell me something about yourself?"

"I'm a college student." Her eyelashes flutter. "From out-of-state." A tragic look glints in her big round eyes. "My father passed away suddenly. So I'm looking for a sugar daddy to support me financially. I've got two years to go before I graduate."

"How much do you want?"

"Three thousand every month." Her tone of voice is matter-of-fact.

"And what will I – I mean, your sugar daddy get?"

"A meet-up every week when I'm free. Movies, dinner, dancing, picnics."

Hot blood pulsates in Kane's loins. "Sex included?"

"No, no sex. Holding hands at the most."

A disappointed smile lines Kane's lips. "Come on, please do your Math. Three thousand works out to seven hundred and fifty per meet-up. No man will pay that amount just to have a date with you without sex. For that price, I can get the prettiest social escort in town."

Liza hikes her chin. "A sugar baby is different from a social escort. She is exclusive to one man."

"Make it two thousand. Four meet-ups per month."

Before Liza replies, a waiter brings them their food. Kane and Liza start to eat, and for a while, there is only the sound of knives, forks and spoons clanging against China plates. *Papa used to tell me that when you're negotiating, the first to speak during silence loses.* Kane swallows his food, scans the other diners in the restaurant and takes a quick drink of his fruit juice.

"Two thousand five hundred, but I want advance payment."

Whoopee! My old man was right! "What guarantee that you won't take my money and run?"

"Why don't you give me two cheques every month? Split the amount – one current cheque and the other, post-dated the fifteenth."

"That sounds a bit fairer." A devilish grin stretches across

Kane's face. "Now that the main issue has been cleared, can we get to know each other better?" A swell of excitement fills his soul. "For a start, where do you live?"

Two years earlier ...

Currently logged on the Internet, Kane types "craigslist Malaysia, sugar baby seeking sugar daddy" into his search engine and taps the "return" key. There are few results and most adverts are by social escorts and freelancers. He tries again using "cracker Malaysia, sugar baby seeking sugar daddy." *Drat! The site has too many ads by transsexuals.* He searches for "sugar baby dating websites" and trawls out a few. The Kuala Lumpur-based female members in the sites don't fit his taste. Finally, he tries "locanto Malaysia, women seeking men in Kuala Lumpur." He finds several advertisers by sugar-babe wannabes and signs up for free membership in the website. *Hot ziggety! There are several ads by woman in KL and Petaling Jaya and I can write to them.* He also inserts his own advertisement under the classifieds heading "men seeking women". *I hope this sugar baby thing can add a breath of fresh air to my humdrum life.*

Three years earlier ...

Kane leans forward in his chair. "Doctor, what's the prognosis for my wife?"

An hour ago, his wife was admitted to a private hospital in Kuala Lumpur for injuries sustained in a vehicle accident.

"From what I see from the MRI report, there're severe injuries to her lower back. These injuries have paralyzed both her legs.

It's likely that she'll be confined to a wheelchair for life." The good doctor adjusts his spectacles. "Also, her sexual, bowel and urinary functions may be affected."

"What!" Kane feels his scrotum shrivel. "Oh, my God!" His palms become sweaty.

The present ...

"I blew quite a big sum on my former sugar baby." Kane takes off his spectacles and blinks. "My biggest mistake was falling in love with her. After one year, I bought her a car and also rented her an apartment." He massages the bridge of his nose. "We also went for expensive vacations in Europe."

I purse my lips. "Any regrets?"

"Under my circumstances, no." He puts on his spectacles. "But the emotional hurt was greater than the financial one. I'm seeking another sugar baby via adverts. This time, I'm not going to make any emotional investment in the relationship. I'll keep her for six months and get a new one later, like changing a car."

"What' s your advice for a potential sugar daddy?"

"F. F. F."

"What does that acronym stand for?"

"Find, fuck, forget." His voice is devoid of emotion.

* * *

Holding a manila card with his name written on it, Steven gazes at the arrival gate of the airport terminal, which is gorging hordes of people. Four fair-skinned women wheeling their luggage bags approach him. One of them steps forward and says, "*Xin chào, tôi là Sươngtừ Sài Gòn* [Hello, I'm Suong from Saigon]."

Steven stretches out his hand. "*Chào mừng đến Kuala Lumpur* [Welcome to Kuala Lumpur]. You speak English?" He grasps the girl's hand lightly.

Suong forms a narrow space between her thumb and forefinger. "Basic English."

Fifteen minutes later, Suong is sitting in the passenger seat next to Steven in his car, which is heading to Kuala Lumpur. In the back seat, the other three Vietnamese girls gawp and point at passing landmarks on the highway. Steven casts his gaze in the rearview mirror and throws a sideways glance at Suong. "Once you check into your rooms, I'm coming round to take photos of all of you. I want to upload your photos on my website by today." Suong turns her head to face her friends and translates what Steven said into Vietnamese.

One year earlier ...

Steven spots a *gweilo* raising his arm to flag him down and he pulls his taxi over to the side. Lugging a briefcase, the man gets into the back seat. "Empire Tower, please use the meter." Steven catches a whiff of after-shave cologne.

"Of course, sir."

Minutes later, the taxi stops at a traffic light and Steven looks in the rear-view mirror. *He looks like a family-man but looks are deceiving.* "Excuse me, sir, travelling alone on business?"

"Yes."

Steven releases the steering wheel and turns his head sideways. "Can I recommend an exclusive social escort for you?"

"No thanks, there're lots of agencies on the Internet."

Steven flicks his gaze to the traffic light and back to his passenger. "My social escort speaks excellent English and is a university graduate from Hanoi." *Poor sucker! She's from a dirty fishing village on the banks of the Mekong River.* "She's a high-class girl!"

His passenger leans forward and places an arm over the back of the passenger seat. "Oh? How much?"

Two years earlier ...

Steven takes a long draw from his mug and puts it down. His pulse pounds in his face like the loud speakers on the stage blasting Cantopop. *Dammit! When can I see the light at the end of the tunnel?* His worries gnaw at his gut like acid burning through rubber.

A fair-skinned young woman walks up to him. "Hello, darling, you want short time?" She is clad in a bare-back top, mini skirt and six-inch heels.

"No, thanks." He takes a deep breath and exhales.

Steven is sitting in a food court at Gelang Road which is a pick-up joint for Vietcong dolls and China dolls. His taxi, two months overdue in HP installments, is parked in front under a tree.

The woman pulls out a plastic chair and sits down. "I'll give you a discount." Her eyes twinkle with hope.

"I've no money and I'm depressed." Steven runs his fingers

through his oily hair. "I just want to get drunk, go home and sleep."

She crosses her legs at the knees and her mini skirt slides upward, revealing milky thighs. "Young men usually have three problems: money, girlfriend or work. What's bothering you?"

"Financial and love problems." The depths of Steven's eyes are filled with hidden sorrows. "I'm thinking how to dig myself out of this deep shithole I'm in!" He slaps a palm on the plastic table. "God is unfair! Always giving the shitty end of the stick to honest decent people."

"Why don't you think of ways to make extra money? If you can become my agent, I'll pay you thirty percent commission." She tosses her gaze at a new customer entering the food court and back to Steven. "In fact, I've a few friends who are also willing to get more business through agents."

"Become a pimp?" Steven's piggy eyes expand bigger from shock. "That's shameful!"

"Money's still money, whether it's white or black!"

Three years earlier ...

A postman enters the front doorway of Steven Bak Kut Teh Restaurant in Kepong, KL, and walks up to the counter. He pulls out a letter from a pile of others wrapped by a thick rubber band.

"Boss, can you please sign for this registered letter?"

Seated at the counter, Steven looks up from the electronic calculator in front of him. "Sure." He pushes a pile of documents aside.

Steven signs on a piece of paper and the postman goes away.

Sitting up straight, Steven tears open the envelope and takes out a document. He unfolds it and starts to read. *Tiew nia ma chow hai! It's a summons! This bloody supplier is just too impatient*!

Tossing the summons aside, he slumps in his chair and rifles his hand through his hair. *Now, where can I cut costs to at least break even?* The fingers of his right hand drum the counter and his eyes flit around the tables in the hall, searching for answers. *Dammit! It's Sandy's fault. She said operating a restaurant would give me respectability. Now, I'm in debt.*

Three-and-a-half years earlier ...
Sandy and Steven saunter along the corridor and stop at the grille iron door of an apartment. Noise from a TV in the inside living room is pouring out into the corridor.

"Good night, Steven," Sandy says, jabbing a doorbell button on the wall.

"Good night, Sandy." Steven turns on his heels and starts to walk away.

Sandy's father opens the grille iron door and calls out, "Excuse me, Steven, I want to talk with you." Stern-faced, he turns to his daughter. "Please go inside, Sandy."

Steven stops in his tracks and looks over his shoulder. "Yes, sir?" He goes to his former spot near the iron grille door.

"I understand you've been dating my daughter for almost six months. You're an honest decent man but I'm afraid I don't approve of you as a prospective son-in-law."

"Huh? Sir, what is it you don't like about me?" Steven's cheeks feel hot. "Is it my financial situation?"

"I'm not a rich man myself so money is not the issue." The old man pauses to release an exhale. "But certain things are best left unsaid." His murky eyes glint with ruthlessness. "So, I don't want to see you here anymore."

Four years earlier ...
A Chinese-style coffin lies in the centre of the hall of the funeral parlour. At the altar stand a photo of the deceased, fruit offerings and candles. Wreaths are stacked against one wall and relatives of the deceased are huddled in a corner, sobbing. Togged up in a burlap of coarse hemp over his clothes, the son of the deceased looks at his watch. "Why isn't the *nam-mor-lor* [funeral-rites priest] here yet?" He wipes away a tear from his cheek. "We should be starting the chanting now."

Steven enters the hall with hurried steps. "Sorry, I'm late – got held up in traffic." He is togged up in a blue robe with a motif of the Taoist *bagua* on its back. On his head is a small black round hat and his feet are shod in fabric shoes that are turned upward slightly. Two musicians start to play the suona and the drum and Steven starts to chant prayers for the deceased.

The present ...
"From a *nam-mor-lor*, I became a bak kut teh-restaurant owner, a taxi driver and, finally, a *kai kung* [pimp]!" Seven releases a hearty chuckle, displaying nicotine-stained teeth. "I'm doing fairly well and have no regrets." He lifts his mug of beer and glugs a deep swallow. "As the saying goes, man proposes, God disposes!"

* * *

I rap my knuckles on Mummy Mandy's (not her real name) office door, hear a muffled "come in" and swing it inward. A blast of air-conditioning tinged with the aroma of rose from an air-freshener greets me. I enter a cramped room and close the door behind me. Seated at a big wooden desk, Mummy Mandy smiles and her eyes crinkle, showing crow's feet. On her desk stands a wine bottle holder in the shape of an old cannon and a Remy Martin ashtray. Several boxes filled with garlands and party hats are placed against one wall on the floor.

Yesterday, I phoned Mummy Mandy to ask the secret of her success as mamasan of Bluey Niteclub (not its real name), located in the city's Golden Triangle. "Training," she said. "Come see me tomorrow and I'll show you. Six p.m. will be fine."

"Ah, Mr. Ewe! You're right on time." Mummy Mandy picks up a sheaf of papers and gets up from her swivel chair. "I'm about to start my training for my new GROs." She rounds her table. "Come, let's sit in one of the karaoke rooms – my girls are there." She leads me out of the room down a hallway and stops at a door with the sign "Opal Room".

She leads me inside and I find myself in a typical karaoke room. There are four GROs sitting at a coffee table, and they are dressed in elegant dresses, nothing slutty. Four pairs of curious eyes wearing purple, copper, brown and orange eye shadow respectively assess me.

Mummy Mandy gestures towards me and pulls an ottoman near the coffee table.

"This gentleman here is a good friend of mine. Just pretend, he's invisible okay? He's just here to observe." She tosses her gaze at me. "You can sit in that corner." As she hands each girl a piece of paper, I settle on another ottoman at the far end of the room.

Mummy Mandy lets everybody settle down. "Let's start the training with a few prompts for general conversation with your clients. First, fuel prices are down – that means reminding your clients to go for a full tank when filling up; there were flash floods in Penang resulting in evacuation of several thousands of people and our country's economy grew in the third quarter. Any questions?" There is silence from the girls. "Now, eventually, some of you will have regular clients who're like boyfriends. At this stage, you'll have opportunities to extract money from him. But only if you play the game right with the right words. So, I've compiled several useful sentences that you should know on the tip of your tongue." Mummy Mandy looks down at the paper in her hands. "Please repeat each sentence five times after me. On your own, you've to practise each sentence until you're fluent in delivery." She scans the faces of her charges. "Ready? First sentence – *I've let you touch my breasts already, so how could you not sponsor my* ... for example, air-fare back for Tet, hospital bill for father's surgery, kid brother's motorcycle, you understand?"

A looker squirms in her seat. "Yes, Mummy!"

Then the four recruits repeat the sentence five times with a tight chorus that reminds me of the Ray Conniff singers! Great Scott! These sex bombs are being groomed to become take-no-prisoners seduction machines!

"There're other variations of the first sentence. Use them

according to the circumstances." I perk my ears as Mummy Mandy utters them:

"*I've given my body to you, so how could you not...*"

"*I've given my youth to you, who's an old man, so how could you not...*"

"*I've rejected men better than you because I truly love you, so how could you not ...*"

"*I am alone and helpless in Kuala Lumpur, so how could you not ...*"

Mummy Mandy clears her throat.

"Next topic is appearance. All men like to be complimented but not all men are good-looking. Here's what to say in difficult circumstances. If he's ugly like a bulldog, say, *Ohh, you're so macho and manly.*"

First, the girls giggle, but the next moment, they utter with passionate seriousness, "Ohh, you're so macho and manly! Ohh, you're so macho and manly! Ohh, you're so macho and manly! Ohh, you're so macho and manly! Ohh, you're so macho and manly!"

The seduction training continues ...

"If he's skinny, say, *Ohh, you're sexy fit and healthy.*"

"If he's wears thick spectacles, say, *Ohh, you're lovable like Mr. Magoo.*"

"If he's short, say, *Ohh, you're a fun-sized dynamite!*"

"If he's fat, say, *Ohh, you're cute like Winnie the Pooh!*"

After the training ends, I bid goodbye to Mummy Mandy and take my leave from the karaoke room. At the main entrance of the nightclub, I draw the split heavy curtains apart and, as I step out, I bump into a young woman wearing a rabbit-ears headband. Her spandex top is straining at her ample bosom and her jorts are revealing lots of creamy white thighs.

"Oops, I'm sorry." I step aside to make way for her.

As she brushes past me, a whiff of her perfume floats to my nostrils, and her fake eyelashes flutter. "Ohh, you're sweet like Mr. Magoo!" Her honey-like voice can attract ants. Phew! Mummy Mandy's effective training induces a gasp of admiration from me.